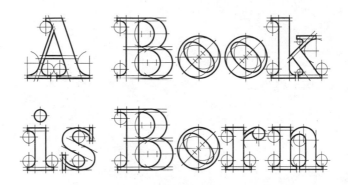

A Book is Born

24 authors tell all

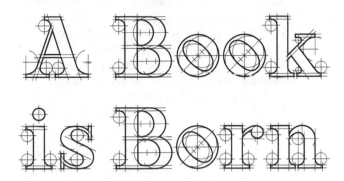

A Book is Born

24 *authors tell all*

CREATED BY **Nancy C. Cleary** WITH CO-AUTHORS:

CHRISTINE LOUISE HOHLBAUM, PAULA SCHMITT, MAUREEN FOCHT,

VICTORIA PERICON, KATHRYN MAHONEY, PAM LEO,

JULIE WATSON SMITH, IRIS WAICHLER, ALANA MORALES,

CAROLINE POSER, MARNA KRAJESKI, TERILEE HARRISON,

ARLENE SCHUSTEFF, NINA MARIE DURAN, KELLEY CUNNINGHAM,

DEBORAH HURLEY, CARON GOODE, CHRISTIE G. CROWDER,

JENNIFER KALITA, SAMANTHA GIANULIS, JENNIFER THIE,

NORMA GARCIA, LEEDA BACON, AND MALONDA RICHARD

Wyatt-MacKenzie Publishing, Inc.
DEADWOOD, OREGON

A Book is Born: 24 Authors Tell All

Nancy C. Cleary with her authors:

Christine Louise Hohlbaum, Paula Schmitt, Maureen Focht,
Victoria Pericon, Kathryn Mahoney, Pam Leo,
Julie Watson-Smith, Iris Waichler, Alana Morales,
Caroline Poser, Marna Krajeski, Terilee Harrison,
Arlene Schusteff, Nina Marie Duran, Kelley Cunningham,
Deborah Hurley, Caron Goode, Christie G. Crowder,
Jennifer Kalita, Samantha Gianulis, Jennifer Thie,
Norma Garcia, Leeda Bacon, and Malonda Richard

F I R S T   E D I T I O N

ISBN: 978-1-932279-50-4 Hardcover
Library of Congress Control Number: 2007931435

Illustrations by Kelley Cunningham, www.kelleysart.com
Editing by Kim Pearson
Jacket proofread by Bernie Panitch
Indexing by Gina Gerboth

Wyatt-MacKenzie Publishing, Inc., Deadwood, OR
www.WyMacPublishing.com (541) 964-3314

Requests for permission or further information should be addressed to:
Wyatt-MacKenzie Publishing, 15115 Highway 36, Deadwood, Oregon 97430

Printed in the United States of America on 50% post consumer recycled paper.

This book is dedicated to our children...

Wyatt, MacKenzie, Jackson, Sophia, Tony, Nick, Phillip, Joseph, Anna, Christina, Natalie, Luke, ?, Tyler, Andrew, Leah, Sage, Finnegan, Ainsley, Bailey Blu, Grace, Darian, Sierra, Mark, Daniel, Gregory, Elena, Stephen, Jackie, Cole, Rachel, Jake, Elijah, Sam, Noah, Nathaniel, Brendon, Lauren, Kennedy, ?, Alex, Zoë, Melia, Ian, Amy, Sammy, Jasmine, Anna, Paul, and Ameerah.

#

JENNIFER BASYE SANDER

"But what is it like?
What is it *really* like to be published?"

I hear that question all the time from the audience at writers' conferences. That seems to be what keeps so many writers going with their projects, the hope that, once they are published, their lives will take a dramatic turn.

A Book is Born answers that question for them. Twenty four women who put it all out there on the page about what it is really like to be published, from start to finish. From coming up with the idea to at long last holding a finished copy in your hand, Nancy Cleary and friends give you an inside look at the process.

No matter where you are now in the process yourself, you'll find new and helpful information, advice, and strategies in this book that will give you a greater chance for success with your own work. Read it. And then get back to work on your own project so you, too, can join the publishing world.

Jennifer Basye Sander is the co-author of *The Complete Idiot's Guide to Getting Published* and author of *The Complete Idiot's Guide to Self-Publishing*, both of which I highly recommend. Jennifer knows all sides of the publishing industry, she is a former Random House senior editor and the author of more than forty books. Jennifer and her husband run Big City Books Group, a book development and publishing consulting firm.

Preface

NANCY C. CLEARY

I learned a lot during the first seven years of running my independent press. My experiences taught me the power of an author's platform; the many sides of distribution; how to land publicity; and especially the reality of what authors feel throughout the book publishing process. The isolation, confusion, pressure, and endless decisions a new author faces can be overwhelming. Wrong choices or unmet expectations can be devastating. On the other hand, the sheer joy, exhilaration, and empowerment an author feels are worth any pain, and may only be truly appreciated by others who have experienced it.

We empower mom writers.

In 2005 I created a membership program, the *Mom-Writers Publishing Cooperative*, which provided writers with what I had learned they needed: author branding, book marketing materials, platform-building, PR consulting, and a support group. I helped them—and they helped each other—plan and execute a seven-month pre-publication marketing campaign for their books which was presented to our distributor for bookstore reps and buyers.

As part of their membership in the co-op I asked my authors to document their journey and respond to questions at each stage of the process. These 24 talented women generously held nothing back, as you will see when you read their contributions.

My goal for *A Book is Born* is to give the writers and would-be authors who read this book the support, answers, and encouragement the members found in the co-op. It worked for them—I hope it will work for you too!

What you'll find in this Book

PART ONE

24 authors tell all

PEEK INSIDE THE MINDS OF 24 PUBLISHED AUTHORS. We laugh that publishing a book is like having a baby—so prepare for the next nine months! Follow us through the conception of the book idea; to why it is so important for mom writers to publish; to sharing the news; pre-natal care (also known as pre-publication marketing); the actual birth; the bling (when baby wins a book award), and through the media successes (baby's name is on a khyron!) See it all through our eyes.

Tech Talk *(from the experts)* & **Tech Tips** *(from the authors)*
IN BETWEEN THE STORIES AND THE PRINCIPLES OF GETTING published you will find technical terms and industry lingo defined, as well as invaluable insider tips and examples.

PART TWO

The Secret & Science to Getting Published

The Four Principles of Publishing
We share the science behind four publishing principles: how to write well, build a platform, pitch, and publish, combined with your own personal passion.

Teach the class, start a club, create an imprint.
What to do next! We'll give you the tools, resources, and opportunities to take the next step into success as a published author.

What you won't find in this Book

This book is not about developing your craft as a writer, or about finding time as a busy mom to write. For professional writers striving for a major book deal, this is just a glimpse of what can be accomplished in the indie world of publishing.

   This book is not about getting rejected, and how to handle it. It is about making a decision to become a published author; to do whatever it takes to turn the manuscript you have labored over into a book. It is a decision to use your energy to move mountains; a decision to put your belief in yourself on the line.

Goals for this Book

If you want to get published...
My goal is for you to imagine yourself as a member of this community of authors, letting them help you envision how you will take each step with *your* book. In Part Two, I have provided you with the knowledge and tools that will help you along through this awesome, magical, overwhelming, and unbelievably fulfilling journey of becoming a published author.

If you are already published...
I hope you feel a sense of camaraderie and shared appreciation with the women in this book. From their experiences may you find new ideas for your own books. The principles in Part Two will be very familiar to you, but still may give you ideas on how to expand on your success.

Send me your publishing questions. It is my goal to guide authors like you through the publishing journey.

Nancy

~ Nancy Cleary, 2007

Table of Contents

CHAPTER 3

Pre-Natal Care

Book Midwifery 73

Morning sickness · Weight Gain · Cravings 74

Tech Talk
What's a **"Publication Date"**? The Bookstore Shelf Dream 77
The Nine-Month Book Birthing Plan 78

Our Marketing Plans 80

Tech Tips — *To Hire a Professional PR Agent, Or Not?* 87

CHAPTER 4

The Birth

Holding my Baby! 89

Beholding our books for the first time 90

Tech Tips — Questions from newbie authors 97
Book Events · Hate Mail & Bad Reviews · Distribution · Endorsements · Bookstore
Signings · Media Follow-Up · Radio · TV · Oprah

Funny Publishing Stats 108

CHAPTER 5

Newborns

Baby for Sale 109

The first few months 110

Tech Talk
Pitch Your Niche 121

Navigating the Amazon Jungle 125

Tech Talk
Making the most of Amazon 127
Discounts · Rankings · Reviews · Bestseller Campaigns

Returns—is something wrong with my baby? 131

APPENDIX

PART ONE

*"When I had my daughter, I learned what the
sound of one hand clapping is—it's a woman holding
an infant in one arm and a pen in the other.*

*"There's nothing natural about motherhood and
there's nothing natural about writing.
In fact, they're both inhuman tasks and what's required
to do them well is unspeakable."*

~ KATE BRAVERMAN
from *A Question of Balance: Artists and Writers on Motherhood*

CHAPTER 1

Conception

Our Fertile Minds

*T*HERE ARE MANY REASONS WRITERS WANT to publish. For a mother the reason is often intrinsically involved with the dreams for her family, as well as not letting go of her own dreams. I posed this question to my authors: How did you conceive your book idea, and what was your intention in publishing it? Through their answers, the co-op members shared their paths to finding the perfect publisher for their babies.

Tech Talks answers the common writer's concern, "Who am I to write this book?" and gives you some information on how to find professional writing support and examples on how to build a platform.

"Chardonnay. No, seriously, that is how I conceived my book idea."

IN THIS CHAPTER

How our book ideas were conceived

Tech Talk
Ghostwriting, Editing, Coaching and Indexing

Finding a Publisher

Tech Talk
Presence and Platform

How did you first conceive your book idea?

NANCY C. CLEARY

In 2005, after seven hard years in the publishing industry, I created a program for mom writers which included an idea for a collaborative book—*this* book. I planned to bring this special group of women through the traditional publishing process together. We would share everything from problems to publicity to profits—and in the end, we would share our stories.

This is the book I would have wanted to read before starting my journey through the perilous publishing world. It is what I want my own authors to read in preparation for what Wyatt-MacKenzie Publishing can do to help them successfully birth their own books. Through this book, I want them to really appreciate what we are capable of creating together.

SAMANTHA GIANULIS

Chardonnay. No, seriously, that is how I conceived [my book idea]. Dinner was in the oven, my first child was playing with Elmo. I had a glass of wine while cooking dinner and my muse visited my conscious food-loving mind. I began pounding away at the keyboard what was in my heart at the time. I found my voice through food, through my children, and through something I guess you could call "wit," that I expressed in an optimistic theme in each essay. So it turns out that Chardonnay, or to be more exact—grapes, was the inspiration for writing my baby *Little Grapes on the Vine*.

IRIS WAICHLER

I was in the audience of my favorite bookstore, listening to a leading feminist author discuss her latest book. She expressed her anger with her doctors because they were ordering her to undergo medical procedures she hated. She described her sense of helplessness, anger, and sadness at the loss of control of her own body. This triggered a stream of memories I had regarding my own struggle with infertility. I tried to imagine how she would have dealt with it.

That was when I tuned out her story and began to focus on mine. I started creating an outline in my head of all the topics that should be addressed in a book on infertility. What information would have helped me in my struggle? What issues did friends have in their infertility battles? What would be the goals of this book? I would want to empower, educate, and give resource information to the millions of people engaged in all stages of infertility. My goal would be to help them feel less alone and reduce their isolation. I wanted them to hear other stories. I smiled remembering a promise I had made at the time of my daughter's birth—if I somehow beat the odds and had a child of my own, I wanted to help others on their infertility journeys. I had led groups and done individual counseling. It seemed a book was a way of reaching many more people on a far greater scale.

By the time I got home I had written the outline for *Riding the Infertility Roller Coaster: A Guide to Educate & Inspire*. I promised myself that I would do the research. It was a topic I felt great passion about and knew intimately on a personal and professional level. My research demonstrated there was a void and that there was room for what I had to say.

CHRISTINE LOUISE HOHLBAUM

Writing a book was never my intention. At least, the first one, *Diary of a Mother: Parenting Stories and Other Stuff*, was an unintended "pregnancy," an accident. It was born out of my frustration as a new mom of two children. Going from being an Ivy League educated career woman to a SAHM was a major transition. I needed a medium to make sense of the Brave New World I had plunged into. Writing was that medium.

My second book, *SAHM I Am: Tales of a Stay-at-Home Mom in Europe*, grew organically. Through the encouragement of friends, family, and a few strangers, I continued writing stories. The initial thought was to attract readers to *Diary of a Mother* through simple vignettes of my new life in Germany. *Diary* ends with our move to Germany, and I felt it would be a unique continuation of the book by starting a newsletter. I entitled the newsletter, or e-zine, "Powerful Families, Powerful Lives" after an article I had written. Soon I realized I had enough material for a second book. In fact, *SAHM I Am* is twice as long as *Diary*. I suppose I had a lot to say about life in Germany with kids!

KATHRYN MAHONEY

I had been writing a humorous column for four years and decided I wanted to put all of these columns into a book. I wanted to document the stories about my children's lives so that we could look back on them someday and laugh. It's true what they say, your children grow up so fast. Plus my memory isn't what it used to be, so having these stories in print is a great way to preserve their childhood. I can relive it when I'm old and senile. *Cracked at Birth: One Madcap Mom's Thoughts on Motherhood, Marriage and Burnt Meatloaf* was the result!

JULIE WATSON SMITH

After I had my son in 2000, I felt overjoyed, overwhelmed, excited, exhausted, and everything in between. Motherhood was everything I wanted but nothing I expected. I also felt isolated. I soon started connecting with other parents. It wasn't long before I formed a play-group, then a community discussion group, and finally I began writing a monthly parenting column called Mommy Hullabaloo.

Mommyhood Diaries was conceived during one of my moments of isolation. I had just had one of "those" days where everything that could go wrong did. My husband came home and—in jest—asked, "What did you do all day?" Not quite grasping the levity in his query—let's see, how should I put this—I screamed like a hormonal banshee. After that brief episode of temporary insanity, he left me to wallow in self-pity while I watched the school of Goldfish crackers drown in my carpet. Is this what mommyhood was going to be like? What was a typical day like for other moms? Were they spending the day at the salon or wishing they were at a saloon? Were they recording the latest top hit or recording the baby's first babble? Were they running businesses or just running their kids to school? Or, perhaps they, too, were watching their own Goldfish and wondering the same thing I was: What do moms do?

In an effort to answer these questions, I decided to eschew house-work and cooking (two easy choices) as well as sleep (not so easy.) I started asking moms I knew—friends, family, women at the grocery store—to describe a typical day in their lives. The answers humbled and inspired me. I started to feel less isolated and more connected.

The book was an unexpected and completely welcome result of the questions and answers provided by the moms. After polling many, it was clear that moms from all walks of life experienced the same ups, downs and unpredictable chaos on a daily basis, and wanted to share their stories with others. I felt confident that *Mommyhood Diaries* would create a maternal sense of community by illuminating both our common bonds and diversities.

CHRISTIE GLASCOE CROWDER

In 1997, I made "Kelly's Freshman Year Survival Manual" for my little sister Kelly when she left for her first year of college. It was a homemade spiral bound book full of do's and don'ts and special sisterly advice for how to get through college by not making the mistakes I did. For years my family said I should try to get it published. I never took it seriously; I just thought my family thought it was a cute and sweet thing to do for my little sister. It was mentioned in passing every time we ran across it when my sister moved back home from college, moved into her own place, moved back home again.

Shortly after my daughter was born I tinkered with that book for Kelly. Then Natalie Holloway disappeared in Aruba. I was furious. Another young girl violated, kidnapped, drugged, and possibly even killed. I wondered where this girl's friends were while this was going on. Did someone ever tell her it's not smart to get drunk and go off with strange men, and in a foreign country no less? Where were their big sisters? Then it hit me, that's it! Someone has got to get to these girls. I am going to be the Big Sister these girls never had and obviously need. That's when I decided to complete *Your Big Sister's Guide to Surviving College*.

ALANA MORALES

I decided to write *Domestically Challenged* on a suggestion from my husband. I am not the typical "S.A.H.M.", so when I started staying home with the kids, I was completely lost. I had no idea what I was doing —how to take care of the house or how to keep my sanity.

I went to the library and checked out every book relating to being an at-home mom. I was disappointed. They were either out-dated, boring, or too religious. There wasn't anything that told me how to take care of the day-to-day stuff, which is what I needed. After complaining to my husband for the umpteenth time, he suggested that I write it myself. So I did.

PAULA SCHMITT

My first book, *Living in a Locker Room: A Mom's Tale of Survival in a Houseful of Boys* was inspired by—who else?—my four boys. After raising all boys for 18 years I decided that I wanted to write a book—a humorous book—illustrated with my stories.

CAROLINE POSER

What prompted me to write *MotherMorphosis* was the most radical change in my life, my pregnancy, was happening, and if I didn't write about it I would likely go insane.

I had been keeping a journal and corresponding with a friend during my pregnancy and after I gave birth to my first son. Sometime following that I started writing columns and articles. I had no clue how to promote them, but I kept writing them anyway. Then I started adding stories. It was about at that time that I realized I was writing a book.

I bought my domain MotherMorphosis.com in October 2001. I remember thinking the name was so perfect, how could it not be taken? I have since trademarked the term.

MAUREEN FOCHT

The sacrifices my father made in caring for my mentally ill mother is what inspired me to publish *Silent Heroes: Courageous Families Living With Depression and Mental Illness*. When I lost my parents, the idea crystallized to dedicate this book to my father and to help other families. I would lay in bed at night and whole paragraphs would jump into my mind. I learned to get up and write it down. That's how it started. I told my husband, "I'm thinking about writing a book." When I discovered Dad left us some money, I realized I had enough to hire a ghostwriter and psychologist to help me.

NINA MARIE DURAN

When many of my friends got pregnant, they came to me for advice, because I had already been a mother for some time. They asked me everything; from the decision "Should I have the baby or not?" to "I had no idea this is what motherhood is like, help me." I started letting them read my journals.

When I had my son Elijah I was 21 years old. All my friends were going out and having fun, and I was still in school, doing an internship, and had a child to support, love and nurture. Every book I picked up for support had a tone of "happy go lucky, motherhood was so happy." My first year was hard. In my book I wanted to tell the truth. *Elijah on My Mind*—this is what motherhood is like.

ARLENE SCHUSTEFF

I started writing this book accidentally. One day I was looking through my daughter Rachael's baby book and realized I had written all these things down—the first time she used a spoon, first time in the highchair, first time on the potty, and while I wanted to remember these things, they weren't as important to me as some of the more unique things she had done. Like the time she told her preschool teacher that she wasn't cleaning up because she wasn't her maid, or the time in line she told a lady she liked her tie-dyed hair. I started compiling a notebook of Rachael's funny moments, and then later for my son Jake. Then it expanded to observations on motherhood, the ways mothers operate in the new millennium, and it became *Peanut Butter, Playdates and Prozac: Tales from a Modern Mom*.

TERILEE HARRISON

I knew I wasn't the only business mom that needed to get help, the only one who was feeling overwhelmed. And I knew there was nothing else out there on the market that appealed to me. Moms trying to juggle everything, just like I was, can find direction in my experiences and those of the successful women I interviewed in *The Business Mom Guide Book: More Life, Less Overwhelm for Mom Entrepreneurs*.

MARNA KRAJESKI

I looked and looked for a book that explored the emotional experiences of military life with a generous dose of humor. When I could never find one, I decided to write it myself. The writer Anne Lamott said, "You must write the book you wish you'd come upon." So I wrote *Household Baggage: The Moving Life of a Soldier's Wife*.

DEBORAH HURLEY

Following my son and daughter's births in 1993 and 1995, I was struck with a severe major depressive disorder. I suffered intensely for over ten years and throughout that difficult time wrote in my journals everything I experienced. It was around 2004 when I felt a strong desire to offer encouragement and hope to others. Because I had battled this all-consuming condition for so long, I learned how to restructure my life around it, make adjustments for it, find purposeful meaning because of it, and become more accepting of the challenges that life threw at me.

I felt that the hope I could offer would be different, more explicate, more genuine and more indicative of what true depression feels like than other books on the market. So I put my pen to paper and began to write. I gathered my journal entries and assembled my painful poems, years upon years of moving agonizing words. I pieced together a unique vision in my head, and I was transformed from a sufferer to a survivor. My poetry became treasures instead of just mere depressing memories, and in my mind I became someone with substance, someone with history and intangible riches.

Fragments of Hope quickly went from a moment's fleeting thought to an absolutely unstoppable mission. I had no idea that *Fragments* would turn into such a heartfelt labor of love. The time felt right and as my heart began to heal, my words began to flow.

JENNIFER THIE

I said to myself, "I am going to write a book." This had not been a life-long dream of mine, but some things in my life had moved me to make this amazing jump into the literary world. I was going for it. I was going to write a book.

First I started jotting down ideas. Then an outline of sorts started to evolve which eventually became *And Then...Came Arthur*. Next came the announcement to my family and friends. "I am going to write a book and you are all going to be in it!" Many were skeptical. As I soon discovered, skepticism would be the biggest challenge of the book itself! I needed to convince my workaholic husband (and a few others who will remain unnamed) that I could pull this off. Sure, I had three-year-old twins. Yes, I worked every day while they went to preschool. No, I had not written a book before. But all that meant was I needed to learn to live on a few less hours of sleep a night. All will still be right in our peaceful little home. Or will it?

MALONDA RICHARD

I conceived the idea of *My Life Isn't Perfect* a couple of months after my daughter Ameerah was born, once I realized that there weren't any books on the market that chronicled the trials and tribulations of a pregnant single mother. Initially I began writing a series of letters, journals and poems for my unborn child so that she would be aware of my experiences prior to her birth. Three years later I had over 300 pages of transcribed journals and a burning desire to get them published.

My intention for writing the book was to reveal several things about myself that I wasn't proud of, in order to evolve. It was my way of saying: "There are no secrets." I truly want other single mothers to know they are not alone in their experiences. I also want my book to be a cautionary tale for anyone who may be thinking of having a baby without being married or in a committed relationship.

LEEDA BACON

Stan and I had been married for over two years before we conceived our son, Ian. We had planned on having a baby soon after we were married but for an unknown reason (some said we were trying too hard) it took longer than anticipated. The same was true with my book, *Be Ye Encouraged!* The conception came after wanting to author a book for many years but not having the time or the patience to embark on such a huge undertaking. But after several life-changing events in 2004, I found myself at home instead of in the workforce where I'd had a demanding job in the funeral industry. I now had the time I didn't have before. For health reasons I began a diet journey, which led me to writing this book that would help, not only myself, but others as well. My original book ideas included a children's book and a novel, but a diet book? That had never crossed my mind until the pounds started melting away and people started taking notice. Many asked me to write down my regimen so they could also lose weight. Thus, my book was born.

PAMELA JO LEO

Over the years (*almost two decades!*) many parents asked me, "When are you going to write a book about this kind of parenting?" A parent in one of my classes even offered to help me write a book proposal to try to find a publisher. We began working on the proposal but our lives got busy and the project got postponed.

A voracious reader myself, I continued to read every new parenting book that came out and I added their pieces of the parenting puzzle to the ones I already had. By the year 2000, I had over thirty articles and I began re-editing to publish in a collection. When I started working on developing a website, I needed a name for the kind of parenting I was promoting, and *Connection Parenting* was born.

In 2005 I decided this was going to be the year that I finally wrote my book. I had the outlines for my "Meeting the Needs of Children" series, sixteen years of experience teaching the series, and over sixty articles to draw from to finally write a book about connection parenting.

As soon as I committed in my heart to getting the book written that winter, the universe threw open every door to make it happen. I had no money to pay an editor but when Caron Goode, who was creating the Academy for Coaching Parents International, heard that I needed an editor for my book, she offered to barter her editing services for my teaching classes for the academy. We did the whole book through email and telephone.

JENNIFER KALITA

As a home office parent who had struggled with how to honor my roles as both a parent and a professional, I saw a real need in the book world for a comprehensive guide to home office parenting success. So many home office parents feel like they are failing themselves, their families and the global economy, and I wrote *The Home Office Parent: How to Raise Kids & Profits Under One Roof* to reach out to those parents with the strategies I had developed for balance and profitability. The entrepreneurial journey is challenging enough before you throw parenthood into the mix, and I saw too many otherwise excellent parents and talented businesspeople giving up their dreams in the name of overwhelm and exhaustion.

DEBORAH HURLEY

"Am I capable of writing a book? Am I a writer? What does it actually mean to be a writer? What if my book becomes a bestseller? What if my book sucks? What if I receive emails from people all over sharing with me how my book has helped them? Who am I? What the hell am I thinking? These are just stupid dreams, aren't they? What if they're not? What if this is a new chapter in my life just waiting for me to write it? What if this chapter changes my entire world and what if this chapter is a stepping stone to an incredible place that I am meant to be? What if I am setting myself up for a huge fall or disappoint-ment? Who am I and what are the chances of me really getting anything published? I want so badly to just forget about this idea and to go about my life. I want to go back to the way things were before I came up with this unsettling thought."

Ghostwriting, Editing, Coaching & Indexing

What if you're not a professional writer? Don't let that stop you from becoming an author. You can develop a team to help.

Ghostwriting is the most comprehensive service, takes the most time to complete, and costs the most money. The ghostwriter may provide the structure for the book, organize all the information, and write all narrative copy, using color, detail, characterization, mood, drama, humor or whatever is necessary to present the material in the most captivating way. They may research information to ensure accuracy. Ghostwriting may entail using already written material, such as marketing copy, website content, audio or video tapes, letters or journal entries, etc. Or the book may be written from interviews only, which the ghostwriter may conduct, tape, and transcribe, then provide narrative flow and storyline. Usually the ghostwriter uses a combination of interviews and materials. Each book is unique so it varies with the book. All manuscripts need editing, so some ghostwriters may include editing with their writing services.

Or, if you have already written the first draft of a book, an **editor** will help you make it better. You should not be offended by the suggestions an editor makes. You are emotionally attached to your book—or you should be. However, editors are more objective. They can often see what you cannot. Even experienced or famous writers need editors to help them smooth, correct, polish, brighten, or fix their manuscripts. Many people think editing means fixing typos and grammatical errors, and that's it. But this is only a tiny part of editing.

Editing may be broken down into three categories: substantive editing (sometimes called deep editing, content editing, or line editing); copyediting (sometimes called light editing); and proofreading.

Substantive editing includes suggestions on how to rewrite or enhance various elements such as organization and structure, clarity and flow, story line, plot, characterization, dialogue, setting, theme, conflict, resolution, balance between light and dark elements, humor, etc. Wholesale changes to your manuscript may be suggested, such as eliminating, moving, or adding sentences, paragraphs or entire scenes.

Copyediting includes checking for accuracy of punctuation, grammar, spelling, tense agreement, style and voice consistency, fact checking, and just making sure the text makes sense. Most copyeditors use reference guides to language usage, such as *The Chicago Manual of Style* or *The Elements of Style* by Strunk and White.

Proofreading also includes checking for accuracy of punctuation, spelling and grammar, but as its name implies, it is often done after the manuscript has been copyedited and is in the design layout stage. This is because proofreaders also check for how the words look on the page. They check for too many hyphenated words per page, or consistency of italics, bolds and bullets, and other elements of style formatting.

A **writing coach** can help you when you are in the middle of writing something and become stuck, or suffer from writer's block. Or you may have a great idea but you don't know how to go about organizing all the information you have, or you just don't know how to get started. A writing coachcoach may suggest ways to move through these challenges. They don't do any writing or editing themselves, but give you ideas on how to do these things for yourself.

Choosing a ghostwriter, editor or writing coach

Choosing a ghostwriter, editor or writing coach is a highly subjective, individual decision. Your book is your baby, and you want your writer to love that baby nearly as much as you do. You need to find someone with whom you can work in harmony. Commonality of mind, similar values, and simple liking can make the process easy and fun.

See if your prospective writer offers a free consultation (either via phone or in person) to discuss your preliminary ideas, share information about the writing process, and to "feel each other out." This meeting is your chance to ask a lot of questions. What does the writer care about? What do they feel their strengths are? What is their process? Have they written other things similar to your book project? Ask to see previous work, if possible. (One of the challenges of being a ghostwriter is that clients are often protected by confidentiality, so there may be some things they cannot show you. But all writers should be able to show you something they have written.) Be aware that writing for others is different than writing for oneself. When ghostwriting, the writer's style should mirror the author's individual voice as closely as possible.

Ask for references. A ghostwriter costs a significant sum of money and a writing project takes months to complete. It's not a trivial invest-ment, so you should check the writer out as best you can. Anyone who cannot give you references may not be a good choice. On the other hand, we all have to start somewhere. If you want to help someone get started as a ghost-writer, and they don't have references yet, you may be able to get a lower price than from experienced ghostwriters.

Excerpted from *You Can Be An Author Even if You're Not a Writer* (Primary Sources Books, imprint of Wyatt-MacKenzie) by Kim Pearson. Kim Pearson is an author, ghostwriter, editor and teacher, and the owner of Primary Sources, a writing service that helps others communicate and preserve their stories, histories and ideas. She has also authored articles, children's stories, and poetry. In addition, Kim has ghostwritten more than 30 non-fiction books and memoirs for individuals, families and businesses, telling of a wide variety of people and covering a broad range of topics. Her classes have gathered high praise from her students. More about the services of Primary Sources and how they may assist you may be found on the website www.primary-sources.com.

Indexing

Depending on book you may need to also hire an indexer. Does your book need an index? If it is non-fiction and provides information readers will want to re-reference at a later date, chances are an index would add value to your book.

Much more technical than subjective, creating an index can be done with software or preferably with a professional who uses their own software. Gina Gerboth of Pueblo Indexing is a passionate indexer who finds sheer joy in the process of gleaning the keywords and names from a book. I call her the information sleuth. Learn more about Gina's services at www.puebloindexing.com.

DEBORAH HURLEY
How does she know? One editing experience

I began to have major problems with my first editor and became terrified that my creation would never come to be. She was extremely critical of my work and suggested that I rewrite massive pieces. She kept insisting that my book was "too somber" and "too depressing." She was adamant that I provide more hope in the beginning of my book. She thought people who were extremely depressed would not want to read about someone else's painful journey. Although I welcomed constructive criticism, it was difficult for me to not feel attacked and I became extremely upset over the editor's consistent negative feedback. Like a protective mother, I strongly felt as if I needed to defend my book's purpose and meaning.

I asked the editor how she knew people with major depression would not want to hear about someone else's angst and suffering? Had she suffered herself and could she speak from personal experience? Was she merely expressing her opinion or did she have information to back up her recommendation?

I asked myself if I should I listen to my editor, make the changes she suggested and possibly risk that my book would not turn out the way I have envisioned it to be. Should I assume that just because she is an editor she knows what she is talking about? Should I care about her opinion and is her opinion what I am asking for?

I let a few days pass before I responded to my editor's last critique and when I did I was confident and secure. I simply stated that I felt she and I were not a good fit. Even though I was right back to square one, now a few months behind on the editing process, and desperately searching for a new editor, I refused to let my dream would slip away. *Fragments* would eventually find the perfect editor.

How did you find your publisher?

These stories of how my authors found me are not meant to glorify Wyatt-MacKenzie Publishing (though I hope they do!) but rather to show you that the perfect publisher for *your* book is out there. These women all happen to be moms and through a string of connected events they connected with me, a publisher with a focus on mom writers.

PAMELA JO LEO

In February of 2005 I got an email from my editor saying, "I think I may have found a publisher for your book. I've told Nancy about you and your book. Check out her website and if you like what you see, call her or email her." I loved what I saw but was too nervous to call. I spent a couple hours that evening composing a brief email to initiate contact.

The very next morning I had an email from Wyatt-MacKenzie Publishing. I was almost too nervous to open it, fearing it was going to be another dreaded rejection. I couldn't believe it when I read, reread, and reread the words, "Yes, yes, yes, I want to publish your book, when can you have it ready?" I shrieked for joy, did the happy dance in the kitchen, and immediately called my mom and my daughters and emailed Caron, my editor, with the happy news.

I committed to having the book written by May for a November release. Now that I had a deadline (I'm a dead liner) I was on fire to write. I still had to work teaching my classes, and I home-school my eight year-old granddaughter, so I wrote late at night, got up early mornings to write, and accepted generous offers of childcare/playdates to have some writing time on weekends. The morning I finished the last line of the last chapter the sun was just coming up. Our rooster was loudly announcing that it was a new day and Pam had just finished her book. I did it! After all these years, I did it. I really wrote a book, my book.

Since there was no one to celebrate with at that hour of the morning (except our rooster) and I was so energized, I wrote a celebration email to all my family and friends telling them my big news: "I did it!" and thanking them for all the love, encouragement, and support.

JULIE WATSON SMITH

Once I decided to publish my book, I shopped around with several agents. While some gave me the standard, "It's not you, it's me" rejection, the overall response was favorable. The downside was that the agents wanted a high percentage of A-list celebrities to appear in the pages of my book. Here was the challenge—most celebrities are reluctant to expose their children to the spotlight, and those who do will only do so for someone they know—or for a high dollar. Knowing that my claim to fame was that my sister dated the son of Darla from the Little Rascals, and I had a few paltry pennies in my savings, I wasn't sure I could meet the agent's expectations. However, I tried. And tried. And tried some more. Feeling slightly deflated and discouraged, I decided to put the book on the back burner to work on additional projects. Two weeks later, I received an email from Wyatt-MacKenzie saying, "Heard about your book. Very interested. Send a proposal and call me." Those few words changed my life.

I had the opportunity to attend a reading and book signing by Mitch Albom, author of *Tuesdays with Morrie.* During his reading, Mr. Albom spoke about how he struggled to capture the attention of agents and publishers with the idea of *Tuesdays*. One agent told him that he had no idea how to write a memoir, no one would read it, and he should stick with sports writing. (The book has now been called the greatest memoir ever written.) But Mr. Albom never gave up. Once *Tuesdays* was published, he trudged through the endless PR parade all authors do—signings at the corner gas station, traveling to Podunk, USA (located right next to the Boonies.) Tired and frustrated, he kept forging ahead anyway. His hard work finally paid off when Oprah offered to turn *Tuesdays* into a movie. The rest, shall we say, is history.

Often as writers (and as wives, mothers, daughters too) we can feel isolated and inadequate. We want to give up—don't! Rather switch gears to rev up your drive. Connect with other writers, brainstorm new marketing techniques, hug your kids or spend an afternoon reading trashy novels so your mind can just go numb for awhile—whatever you do, don't give up. Who knows? Your big break might be just around the corner.

DEBORAH HURLEY

I was absolutely unwilling to give up on my dream of being published so I persistently read books, researched, asked questions, made phone calls and prayed. Feeling determined yet a bit hopeless at times, one day I picked up a magazine and read a two-page article about a woman in Oregon who had her own publishing company. Her mission was to empower mom writers and assist them in fulfilling their dreams of becoming published authors. The more I read about this business mom in Oregon the more hopeful I became.

With excitement running through my body I emailed Nancy Cleary explaining who I was, where I had been, and where I longed to be. I shared my dream of becoming an author, my mission to help other women who were suffering with depression, and how I was beginning to believe that stay-at-home moms did not have the opportunity to share their gift and their passion of writing with the world. Nancy kindly emailed me back acknowledging the importance of my goals, that my time was possibly now and that my gift was real! After a few emails and telephone conversations, Nancy welcomed me into her co-op group. She believed in my story, in my capabilities, and in my book.

I had completely lost my appetite and I simply could not sleep. I continuously woke up through the night, pinching myself and wondering if it was actually true. I had wanted to become an author for so long and now that it was going to happen, it felt so surreal. I was afraid to tell people because I thought that once I did, I would wake up from my dreamlike state only to realize that it had all been one . Instead I stood in my kitchen by myself and with tears of joy and tears of hope streaming down my face, I softly proclaimed, "I am going to be an author!"

JENNIFER THIE

"Are you going to try and get it published?" they asked. "Well sure, I mean I guess so." I would tell them. My response soon turned into, "Hell, I really have no idea."

Thus began my quest: finding out how everyday people get published. I already knew that you did not just simply send your book to any big-name publishing house. So where does someone find out how to get published? Online, I was inundated with information about publishing your first book. There were an unlimited number of guides to finding the top publishing company and services filled with questions like: "What kind of book are you trying to get published?"–"Trying to find that niche reader?"–"Do you want one-on-one help from the experts?" and then there's "Ten Things That Only I Can Tell You About Getting Published for only $199.99." It was all there. Out of all the information, it boiled down to: A; self publish or B; hire an agent to shop the book around to publishing houses. At this point I threw in the towel and decided to revisit the publishing quandary when I got closer to finishing the book. Write first. Publish later.

I consider good writing a skill and those possessing this skill to be truly gifted. I am not one of those people. This became readily apparent as I tried to turn my story into words, sentences and paragraphs. The problem was there was no cohesiveness or structure. My dyslexia was not helping. I wanted my thoughts to flow seamlessly into well-formed and interesting sentences. I wanted to create art. My ideas sounded very good, I thought, but my writing seemed scattered. It was missing that rhyme and rhythm that makes a reader want to keep turning the pages. Since I imagined that creating reader interest is somewhat crucial to the whole book concept, I knew I needed to get some help.

I began to search for an editor, someone who had written a book or two, as well as done some editing and knew what they were doing. The first professional I hired seemed qualified and interested but did not work out. Ditto the second. These two failed attempts consumed six months of my attention and energy. I became discouraged. Thankfully, I did not give up and found the perfect match on my third try.

Whipping my book into shape has taken a long time but it is almost done. The most important lesson I learned: never give up on your dream of writing a book. It took me two years to write a rough draft and six more months to find the right someone to help me make it come to life. And what is my pay off in the end? Well the wonderful woman who I hired to help me write my book told me about Wyatt-MacKenzie. She thought my book might be a good fit with them. I truly lucked out.

It is not often that wonderful little gifts come into our lives with such a perfect fit. When the opportunity came to work with Nancy Cleary and the women of the MWPC I only had one answer–Yes! I knew that most other writers were initially rejected by publishers once, twice, maybe more times before succeeding. My happy ending of getting published may seem a bit "too happy" to believe. It took me several weeks to tell family and friends that the book that I have been working on since 2003 was not only about to be finished, it was going to be published!

CHRISTIE GLASCOE CROWDER

I did some research on publishers and agents. I even took a class on how to get published and the whole process terrified me. I had no idea how to go about convincing these people on paper that my book would be a bestseller since the "bottom line" is all big publishing houses look at when considering a piece. Then I researched self-publishing, figuring that would be a better, or rather easier, option. It turned out to be an expensive option that I could not afford. In March 2006, I discovered a magazine called *total 180!* and in it was an article about Nancy Cleary and Wyatt-MacKenzie Publishing. I learned about Nancy's Mom Writers Publishing Cooperative that specialized in publishing books written by authors who were mothers. I browsed her website and looked at all of the wonderful women in the cooperative and their intriguing books. I wondered if Nancy would be interested. I took a chance and sent an email with that very question. Within the hour, she wrote me back asking me about my project. I described the book, its origin, and my inspiration for writing it again. Less than 30 minutes after I hit "Send" my phone rang. It was Nancy on the other end saying, "I love it! I want to do this. Can you have it finished by September?"

CHRISTINE LOUISE HOHLBAUM

SAHM I Am seemed to be doomed to failure from the start. It actually went through three publishers who initially accepted the work and then, for a variety of reasons, did not publish it. The first was an Internet scam artist who posed as a boutique publisher. Ironically, he was really encouraging and motivated me to complete the manuscript. Even though he was painfully dishonest, I am grateful for the impetus his initial contact provided. Without him, *SAHM I Am* may never have been born!

The second publishing house saw too many obstacles in distribution for me. Since I live in Germany, they felt it would be best for me to find a larger house. I even tried to get a literary agent to represent me. Twenty minutes after I received an email rejection letter, Nancy Cleary emailed me to ask about my plans to publish *SAHM I Am*. She had a new publishing concept in the works, born out of her success with another mom author, Jen Singer of *14 Hours 'Til Bedtime*.

Nancy had interviewed me a year prior about *Diary of a Mother*. She even featured it on the cover of her *Mom's Business Magazine*. Impressed with her work, I couldn't believe she approached me! She was the midwife I had longed for all this time. While it seemed no one else believed in my project (except the scam artist on the West Coast), Nancy stood by me and my writing. It was the first real step towards autonomy as an artist, and I had the backing to make the book a reality.

IRIS WAICHLER

I had real difficulty convincing publishers that infertility was a viable topic to be considered for publication. I had previously published a book in 1988 called *Patient Power: How to have a say during your hospital stay*. This experience was different in several ways. Five of the publishers I contacted this time had gone out of business. It was a much tighter market to break into now. Because my book was for a specialty population many publishers did not want it. Some publishers told me there was already enough material out there in spite of the fact my book looked at topics I had not seen elsewhere.

It felt really good when I finished my book and it had been edited. It had all the elements I hoped it would have. I knew it had the potential to help and touch the lives of many people going through infertility. That had been my goal all along. My concern was how to reach these people in the best possible way. After reading an article in the *Chicago Tribune* about a publisher for mom writers, I wrote Nancy Cleary about my book and she immediately understood the potential and the population I was reaching out to. I was elated.

When Nancy invited me to join the co-op, I was just thrilled. She explained all of the support available and the experts she could link me up with to fill in the missing pieces. I knew I had a good shot at making my dream of having this book published become a reality. It was a great feeling.

MAUREEN FOCHT

I knew it was extremely difficult to find an agent and a big-name publisher, and I'm not the kind of person who can persevere and keep sending out letters month after month knowing it's futile. With the new publishing service companies using print on demand, I knew I could get my book published that way. I started down that road and then I heard that bookstores will not order print-on-demand books because they were non-returnable. Luckily, my ghostwriter knew about Wyatt-MacKenzie who had a unique program providing traditional publishing.

LEEDA BACON

Since so many people were interested in my diet ideas, I thought publishers would be too. Wrong! As I sent out proposal after proposal to different publishers, I received form letters stating that the book didn't fit their current "lists"—I'm sure they didn't even look at that proposal from this first-time author.

Then I heard about Wyatt-MacKenzie Publishing and emailed a query letter expecting to get the usual response, or no response at all. Instead I received an encouraging email from Nancy Cleary saying that she was excited about my ideas. Wow! Someone was willing to talk to me! We emailed and spoke on the phone several times before I made the decision to join the Mom Writers Co-Op. Although it's been years since I gave birth to my son and daughter, I felt I had experienced a lot of the same birthing challenges while writing my book; sometimes I even wondered if the book would ever be born. Wyatt-MacKenzie nursed it along.

Creating the book caused overwhelming joy and excitement, just as when our first child was conceived, but I also had concerns. Would he be healthy and have all of his fingers and toes? (Have I forgotten to include something integral to the book?) Would he crawl, then walk and finally run when he's supposed to? (Will the book do well when it hits the bookstores and continue to have an audience?) Not knowing the future of my "baby" is both frightening and exhilarating, but I wouldn't miss this for the world.

KATHY MAHONEY

When I began researching publishers I was fortunate enough to contact Nancy Cleary at Wyatt-MacKenzie Publishing. I read about her Mom-Writers Cooperative in the *Boston Herald* and recognized it was a perfect fit, both personally and professionally. Come to find out, Nancy's sister lives in my town in Massachusetts.

CAROLINE POSER

I self-published in 2002, but that wasn't the same as getting the book out into the world. I sold quite a few copies, but it was all direct sales and while I had figured out everything from ISBN numbers to bar codes to registering with the Library of Congress, I just couldn't figure out the distribution part. I learned about Wyatt-MacKenzie through an author who lives in my town that had just been published by Nancy. I pitched her a new edition idea, and she wanted it!

MARNA KRAJESKI

I had several nibbles by publishers. One wanted to turn it into a helpful guide with information on how to pack boxes, relocate, keep your records in order during a move, etc. I told her those books were already out there; I wanted to do something different. If you'll forgive the generalization, a "how-to book" is a very masculine way of approaching life. You know how, when you talk to your husband about something of an emotional nature, he'll interrupt by saying, "Here's how you fix that." Well, maybe I just want to talk about it, and that makes me feel better. Maybe I don't want you to cut to the chase with a diagnosis. Just listen for awhile. For women, talking and listening is very therapeutic and that's what I was trying to do with *Household Baggage*—facilitate a little dialogue.

The second interested publisher ultimately opted out because they hadn't had much success with their narrative non-fiction in the past. For my book to succeed, they felt it needed a lot of publicity resources and money which they didn't have. Darn! But it also points out another valuable lesson—on to the next publisher/agent until you find the right one. I started out with a file folder of rejection notices. Eventually that got so large that I had to graduate to a box.

How did it feel when I found a publisher? It was a joyful relief. I not only found a publisher, I found in Nancy someone who understood the hearts of women, the powerful need for sharing and connection mothers have, and willingness to take on the "stepchild" of publishing— emotional, memoir-type, narrative non-fiction.

ALANA MORALES

I have not acquired the numerous rejections that many writers have. I got decent feedback from several agents I queried, but none would represent me. I read a stat today that said that 80% of people in America want to write a book. So I guess that means that I'm doing better than 80%. Does that put me in the top 20%? Regardless of how the book is received by others, I am thrilled that I finished a book and found the Mom-Writers Publishing Co-Op. I am actually an author! How many people can say that?

NINA MARIE DURAN

I had no idea what I was doing. I went to amazon.com, clicked on "parenting" and looked through hundreds of books. On each I scrolled down to see who the publisher was, and kept writing them down. Over and over the name Wyatt-MacKenzie kept coming up. It was one of the first websites I looked up and I was in awe of the other women I saw there. When I called Nancy I was able to speak with her, every time, that was amazing. I had found my publisher.

ARLENE SCHUSTEFF

After I had written some vignettes and parodies and lists, I looked at them and thought, this would be a very funny book. I didn't know what approach to take so I went to the bookstore and spent many hours looking through books with titles like *How to Publish Your Book* and basically got really discouraged. It was a downer. Unless you were already a published author, you couldn't attract the attention of a publisher— kinda like a catch-22. Then I was in a Yahoo listserv group for writers and someone in that group mentioned Wyatt-MacKenzie. I went to the website and saw the other mom authors and got really excited. But then the lawyer's wife in me said, this is too good to be true. So I shelved it in the back of my head. Later I was on the same list again and another writer started talking about Wyatt-MacKenzie. So offlist I emailed her and asked, "Is this too good to be true? Is this for real?" and she convinced me that it was real and suggested I call Nancy. The rest is happily published history.

MALONDA RICHARD

I was completely aware that many talented writers with compelling stories might never find a publisher to help support their dream. I had already experienced so much rejection in the entertainment industry and I wasn't about to experience more rejection with a book that is, without a doubt, my baby.

I felt like I won the million-dollar lottery when I signed with Wyatt-MacKenzie Publishing. I was sitting on top of the world for over a week. I had been surfing the net and kept coming across several sites with mothers who were really making strides in the motherhood movement. Somehow that search led me to Wyatt-MacKenzie and from the first moment that I talked with Nancy I knew that I was on to something very special. A month or so later I was blessed enough to become the 24th mom author of the Wyatt-MacKenzie Mom-Writers Cooperative. The fact that WM is a small publishing house that works like a big publishing house is definitely a plus for authors like me. I don't have to worry about just being another author on the roster.

The thing that impressed me most about WM is the fact that Nancy brings a spiritual component to each and every one of her projects. In my mind Nancy is the equivalent of a midwife or doula. She is a woman who will give me the knowledge and tools that I need to give birth to a magnificent baby (book).

SAMANTHA GIANULIS

Oh Goodness, I have been lucky. A whole list of connected events transpired. I stumbled on to a website where one of my essays was given a home, which gave me the opportunity to write for the website owner's book, which was published by Wyatt-MacKenzie. Then an article I wrote for *total 180! magazine* was only pages from a great article about the same publisher, Wyatt-MacKenzie. Then I found *Mom Writer's Literary Magazine* which accepted another one of my essays and a poem, and then offered me a column and I realized the founder was also published by Wyatt-MacKenzie.

I discovered I was in an "inner circle" of amazing mom writers. I thought perhaps Wyatt-MacKenzie would be interested in my collection of mommy-centric food-based essays. And they were! Lucky me.

JENNIFER KALITA

I contributed some mom entrepreneur success tips to a book compiled by another author of my publisher's, and then I gave a teleseminar to all of the women in the book about how to put the book to work and maximize their contributions by using it to boost their own business PR. The publisher was on the call, who then reached out to me asking about titles I had in development. I was not at all sure that I was ready for the publishing journey, but I knew enough about publishing to know that publishers don't often come to you, so I jumped in. If I had waited until I knew everything about publishing, I may have never published at all. Just like when you're deciding if you're ready to start having kids, if you wait until you know everything about parenting, have the "right" house and all the money you think you'll need, you'll never have them.

DEBORAH HURLEY

"What makes your story unique?" "Who are you, have you ever had anything published before?" "The topic of your book does not interest us at this time, Good luck." " You're just a housewife?" "Some people try for years and years to get something published and are unsuccessful." " This topic has already been written about." "You do realize that this may never be published, don't you?"

As much I wanted to believe in what I was writing I couldn't help but think that I had fooled myself into believing that my poetry and writing was worthy of publication. I felt as if I was on an emotional roller coaster and everyone in my house was beginning to feel the ups and downs. I asked myself if I was able to go after what I wanted but to not have it affect my entire life.

Beds were not being made, laundry was not being washed or folded, and dinner had become a hassle instead of something that I usually loved to create. I spent hours upon hours in front of my computer emailing, rewriting and researching, I realized that my family had taken a back seat and because of that, I began to feel anxious and even depressed at times. I laughed at the irony. I had written a book on depression and I was feeling anxious and depressed over the stress of trying to have it published. I knew in my heart that this was an amazing adventure for me and that I needed to find a way to make and keep it a happy one. So... filled with anxiety, euphoria and even mild depression, I asked myself one question only: Did I believe that I had something unique that the world just could not live without? My answer was "Yes."

Having Presence

Publishers are only interested in an author's "platform"—the answer to the question, "Who am I to write this book?" Your **platform** equals the powerful combination of what you stand for, what you are passionate about, and who you are as a person, multiplied by who cares about this message *and* how many ways they hear, see, and feel it. You can build your platform by the strength of your message and the unforgetability of your image. (You'll learn more about presence in the Presence Principle in Part Two.)

An **author brand** is one way to quickly show who you are. A brand conveys your personality and what is memorable about you, visually and verbally. Once you develop the look of your brand you will convey it in all mediums to have the most impact.

Web Presence - The banner on your blog, the design of your web site, emails, blog comments, syndicated columns, newsletters—everything you do online has your image, tagline or signature.

Printed Marketing Materials - the memorability of your business card, postcard, bookmark, poster and advertising is what will keep you on the minds of customers and media.

Promotional Items - giveaways, journals, T-shirts, Coffee Mugs, Travel Cups, Calendars, Totebags, all emblazon with your brand will build your visibility and give customers and media a great "experience" with your brand.

Often authors will spend their Advance on branding materials and PR. Having a consistent, professional look will make an impact to reviewers, reporters, producers and customers.

On the following pages are some of the brands created for the co-op members. As you look through the materials imagine how you can create an unforgettable brand of your own.

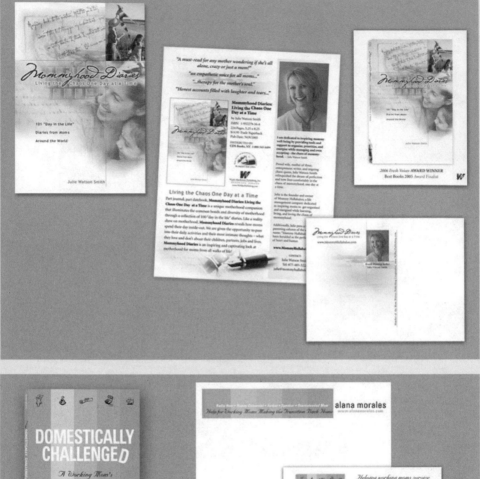

LEEDA BACON

What's in a baby's name?

Wow, your dream of becoming a mommy is coming true. You're expect-ing! But expecting what? A boy? A girl? A book? And what will you name it? In the beginning stage, you delight only in the fact that it is really happening. Then someone asks you, "What are you going to call it?" The name that you choose for that cute, cuddly bundle that demands all of your time will be his or her identity for life. It can give him significance or insecurity. It will make him stand out or fade into pale. The name you select should build his character as he matures, not giving opportunity for others to criticize or ridicule. It should express qualities of excellence, dignity and courage. A name becomes who you are and it can make or break a spirit. It could be the differ-ence between success and failure. Whoever thought that choosing a name for your precious little one could be so important? But it is.

CHAPTER 2

Sharing the News

I'm Having a Book!

*A*NNOUNCING TO FAMILY AND FRIENDS that you are going to have a baby—whether biological or paperback—can be met with mixed responses. Some will support you, while others will doubt your ability. I asked my authors to share the reactions they received when they shared the news with friends and family that a book was on the way.

Tech Tips has a Q & A from the co-op emails. Tech Talk address the sonogram—a picture of the upcoming miracle, an advance peek at the life grow-ing inside you—the book cover and advance review copy.

"The funny thing about telling my friends and family that I was going to be a published author is they automatically thought I would achieve Alice Walker or Terry McMillan status overnight."

IN THIS CHAPTER

Sharing the News of the Upcoming Book

NANCY CLEARY

My cousin Kate stopped by to visit us recently. Since her move from Oregon to work as a bartender in Vegas we see her once or twice a year. When I told her I was finally publishing my book she said, "YOUR book? Yours, not someone elses? YOURS? After publishing hundreds of others' you're finally publishing yours? OH MY GOD! What's it about?"

"It's about publishing those hundreds of others."

"Oh, cool."

JENNIFER THIE

It was in early spring 2003 when I decided to turn a short story I wrote for my "Mothers of Multiplies Club" into a book. I was feeling so pumped up from all the amazing feedback I received from the short story, I was sure everyone would be thrilled to hear the exciting news that I, Jennifer Thie, was going to jump into the book writing game! Boy, was I wrong. It seemed the people closest to me all had something to say, and it wasn't all positive. Comments like, "When are you going to find the time to write?", "You have never written a book before," and "The subject is boring, no one will want to read it," and, of course, "You know most people don't get published." And the biggest cynic of the bunch was my husband. So even before I put my fingers to keyboard, I was getting the big thumbs down from the people I needed support from the most. I understood why they were being so hard on me (especially my husband)—you hate to see the ones you love fail or be hurt. But I also knew in my heart that my drive to write a book was so strong, I had to block their bullshit concerns and push forward. Lucky for me, I have always been one of those people who work best when an adversary tries to shut me down. I come back swinging, or in this case, writing!

The worst came when my husband and I were out on a "date night," which, after having kids, happened infrequently. It was a perfect evening; sitting outside at our favorite Italian restaurant where only five years earlier he proposed to me. Everything was just lovely, that is, until I brought up "the book."

I told him that I was moving forward with the book, despite the fact that the story was, in his words "unreadable and boring." Not to mention the cost of me hiring an editor—I am profoundly dyslexic and knew

I would need help. The eating utensils hit the plate and that was it. Our perfect evening turned into the date from hell! Let's just say the argument lasted long enough for him to tell me, once again, that the book would be a waste of time and money, and a lot of heartache. So, I did what any good wife would do—I told him to shove it, put my napkin down, grabbed my handbag and started my walk home. Now, in my husband's defense (before you go off thinking he is the biggest jerk in the world), I could kind of see where he was coming from. The story I was going to write would not be a book he would feel compelled to pick up in a bookstore; he is a war story, horror book kind of guy. I would have to hire an editor and at the time I thought I would most likely self-publish. I had no idea what the cost would be for all of that. So in that respect, he was making some very valid arguments. By the time I got home (less then a mile from the dinner disaster) he was waiting out in front of the house with lots of apologies. We made up before we got into the house. I did let him know that I was moving forward with the book with or without his support. Happily, I can say, we have not had a fight about it after that night, and, he has been a big help as well.

So even before the book begin to take form, I was learning some pretty hard lessons about finding support for my newfound passion. And after that entire negative pooh-pooh from some of my "non-believing" loved ones, I better produce or I would feel like a great big fool.

CAROLINE POSER

The weird thing about telling my friends I was going to be published is that they didn't seem all that enthusiastic. New friends and acquaintances were more interested. It became a self-esteem deflator, almost to the point of my not wanting to mention it. But I have come to embrace my identity as an author and to hand out my business cards shamelessly. It actually gave me a tremendous amount of credibility in my corporate role, to which I was promoted exactly at the same time my book was released (when it rains it pours.) My manager, a man, has read my book (about pregnancy) and enjoyed it!

LEEDA BACON

My family has been my biggest support system through this whole process, from conception to publication. They are my cheering section. My daughter, Amy, who lives in North Carolina, thought a diet book that offers an easy to follow, simple to implement regimen will help many busy moms and was thrilled when I told her I had finally found a publisher. My husband, Stan, who put up with me getting up in the middle of the night when I had a brilliant idea that had to be jotted down, was happy that Wyatt-MacKenzie would be my publisher, but concerned that the marketing demands might be overwhelming. I thought it was sweet that he was concerned but then I thought that he should know me well enough to know I love a good challenge.

I received two great responses after the announcement that my book would be born (published); one from a close family member and the other from the person who edited my book. My sister Sherry said with excitement, "Go for it!" And, my editor, whom I had never met, wrote this on the manuscript, "Excellent book!" Positive remarks really encourage you.

JULIE WATSON SMITH

My family would support a decision for me to sell spit-up perfume if that's what I wanted to do. With that said, they are all excited about having a published author in the house, and even happier that I'm not selling any putrid wares. As for my kids, they are still very young so they don't really know the difference. They did think it was pretty cool to see me on a book jacket and on TV. Other than that, I'm just mom, and I'm still fishing those Goldfish out of my carpet on a daily basis.

I am usually the type of person who you can read like a book, and I'll shout news from the mountaintops. This was one of those deeply personal moments, though, that I wanted to selfishly savor by myself for a few days. I did, however, share the news with my late Vans-wearing, tank-top clad grandmother during my daily meditation. I like to think that she danced a little jig in Heaven when she heard the news. After a few days, I shared the news with my very proud husband.

Probably the most memorable response was my mom who kept saying "Really? Really? Really?" She gushed about how happy and proud she was and gave me the best accolades a daughter could hear. And then promptly hung up with nary a goodbye to spread the news to all her friends.

ALANA MORALES

Does my family support me being published? Yes! My husband was a little skeptical, but now he is my biggest cheerleader. I am very thankful to have his support and couldn't imagine it any other way. He is helping me think of marketing ideas, which is great. I can't imagine what it will be like when we see the book for the first time. He gets excited seeing my picture in the newspaper with my column in it, so I can't wait to see his expression when there is a book with my name on it.

I didn't really tell a lot of people because it seems that people like to hear about stuff that is "normal" and publishing a book is not the norm. Many people didn't even get what I meant and were surprised to hear that I had written a book. I'm not sure how many interpretations there are of "I have a book coming out" but apparently there are a few that I didn't know about.

My feelings about having a book? Sheer terror. There is so much to do that I don't want to leave anything out and I don't want to feel like I'm not putting 100% into it.

CHRISTIE GLASCOE CROWDER

The funny thing about telling my friends and family that I was going to be a published author is they automatically thought I would achieve Alice Walker or Terry McMillan status overnight. In their eyes, I am automatically a bestselling millionaire. My father has already planned his retirement so he can live off of my earnings. Though I appreciate their enthusiasm and expectations, I do have to occasionally bring them to reality which is—the money I will make from each book that sells in a store will barely get you a soda out of a machine, well maybe a can of Sam's Choice cola at Wal-Mart. The point is that they are happy and supporting me and can't wait until they have one in their hands!

I don't exactly remember who I told first, but I just remember that after I stopped running around my house screaming like a banshee, I made a lot of phone calls. My husband, my mother, my sister, my friends, then I think I sent out a broadcast email to catch everyone else at once. Everyone responded with the same enthusiasm and asked when they could quit their jobs!

IRIS WAICHLER

My husband is a writer and he was incredibly supportive. He helped edit the book and totally understood what I was doing and what I was up against. He also understood the content of the book and his input and ideas were invaluable. He helped me put the contents into perspective.

My daughter is only five but thinks it is very cool. My family has been extremely supportive and encouraging.

My friends in my daughter's playgroup were quite wonderful. I used some of their stories in my book. They wanted autographs and offered to throw me a party.

I had the earlier experience of publishing a book but that was very different from now. My mother was dying at the time and so I was totally disengaged from what was going on in my book. I remember opening my first royalty check back then and feeling little emotion. This time is entirely different. I have been active in terms of the marketing and I'm excited about participating in putting all the pieces together. Seeing my name on Amazon felt great. Getting an endorsement for my book from a person I really admire and respect caused me to jump up and down like a little kid.

CHRISTINE LOUISE HOHLBAUM

My first book, *Diary of a Mother*, came out when my children were two and four. For the longest time, they both called it "diarrhea of a mother". Luckily, they've outgrown baby talk. To be honest, the first thing they said was, "Look, mom's got a diarrhea!" Thanks, guys. I love you, too.

My husband was rather amused at first. He thought it was a passing fancy until he saw me working late at night and up at dawn to network with other writers, journalists, and the media. "You have a radio interview at 4 pm Los Angeles time?" he asked once. I could see him doing the math in his head. "That is 1 am our time!" Living in Germany can have its disadvantages I cheerily told him, then set the alarm for 12:45 am. My most memorable response was my mother. "I always knew you would famous!" she howled. It was delightful.

PAULA SCHMITT

The first person I told the good news to was my husband, Tom. After I hung up the phone with Nancy, my publisher, I ran into the other room of our home and hugged my husband while jumping up and down. He was so happy for me that he lifted me up into the air, twirled me around, and gave me the biggest hug ever. This was such a thrilling and special moment for me and it was wonderful to have someone to share it with.

For the long road ahead...I knew the next six months would be filled with uncertainty and a lot of work. I also knew that I had the support of my family and friends and that Nancy would be there to guide me along the way.

KATHRYN MAHONEY

My family is 110% supportive. My husband is very encouraging and also a good sport since a chapter of my book is dedicated to him and his imperfections! He wanted me to follow my dream and was with me every step of the way. My two children were young enough to be proud and also young enough not to really realize how many of my stories poked fun at their foibles. Something tells me they might not be quite as supportive when they're teenagers and actually understand what mommy told the world about them. But, then again, maybe that will be the ammunition for my next book!

PAMELA JO LEO

When I began telling people I was getting published a lot of them said "It's about time". This has been my dream for so many years. Everyone knows my story of getting Nancy's email with her response, "Yes, yes, yes."

My granddaughter's reaction to the book was interesting—there had been so much of, "Grandma, do you have to work on the book today?" One of my greatest memories was the day when I was writing and she was needing me and said, "Grandma I think you're writing more about connection parenting than doing it." I pushed the keyboard away.

MARNA KRAJESKI

My sisters and parents reacted about the same way they did to the news of my two real pregnancies—with remarkable indifference. I think they thought it was pie-in-the-sky and that I would never actually accomplish it. My mother-in-law lectured us that it would be bad for Paul's military career! (So shut up and scrub the kitchen floor, Marna.)

MAUREEN FOCHT

My husband is wonderful. He has always been extremely supportive of almost anything I want to do. I guess not if I ran away with another man, but other than that! I did worry about my brothers because they have not come to terms with my mother's mental illness as much as I have. I wondered how they would react. But eventually they were okay with it, at least that's what they told me. If they felt any different, I didn't know. I never heard any negative comments.

TERILEE HARRISON

Everyone was so excited. They were all so happy and so surprised I found a publisher so quickly from the time I said I was going to publish a book. Everyone thinks they have a book inside them, and no one could believe I had actually done it.

ARLENE SCHUSTEFF

How did people react when I told then I was going to be published? Disbelief. My family and my friends were really excited for me. They were surprised that I had actually accomplished this. They were a little numb to the fact though since my articles had been published in numerous newspapers and magazines. My name was out there. It wasn't a big deal to them.

NINA MARIE DURAN

When I first said "I'm going to write a book," I got laughter. And then when I found a publisher they said, "Oh my God you're serious?" Everyone slowly became excited for me. People were pretty shocked. My dad is a "once I see it I believe it" kind of guy. Some had mixed emotions, asking me, "You're going to lay yourself out for the world to see?" I told them if it could help one mom, one young mom, one single mom, it would all be worth it.

SAMANTHA GIANULIS

I was as humble about the news that I was being published as possible—reserved even. I almost believed it was too good to be true. I only told people who would be directly affected-family and friends who would be helping, and then casually told others as I came into contact with them. My hubby said, "No way!" on the phone. My mom said to everyone, "Have you heard? Have you heard!"

DEBORAH HURLEY

Some people didn't understand. They said things like, "How much do you have to say?" Many people weren't on board at first. There was a lot of jealousy, expressed in negative comments. Instead of saying, "Wow, you did good," they threw another obstacle in my way.

My husband and children were extremely supportive all throughout the process though.

MALONDA RICHARD

My entire family supports the upcoming birth of my book but I know it won't be real for them until they actually see the book published. Once I had my publishing deal I immediately decided to have the book released on my Grandmother Christine's birthday as homage to her and her legacy. My mother was the first person that I called and, as usual, she was very happy for me. Next I called my family and friends and told them and everyone was ecstatic about the news.

JENNIFER KALITA

What was the reaction when I shared the news? "Finally!" I had been coaching many home office entrepreneurs and speaking on these issues for years, so my support circle was thrilled when I finally put these formulas down in a book.

Tech Tips were collected from the co-op Yahoo email list. They were the questions I found most compelling, with their multitude of responses.

Should I use my real name?

Q: *I have a big question. I am writing a very personal, biographical book. Should I use my real name? My husband's real name? My kids' real names? My friends' real names? You get the idea. In many ways, I feel that it would seem dishonest if I used fictitious names. However, since I have never done this before, I am guessing that I do not know what the potential pitfalls and risks are in using real names. So there it is. Any advice from those with experience would be greatly appreciated. Thanks.*

A: I say use the real names. I do agree that if using your children's names and husband's real name would have a negative impact on their lives then maybe that's something to think about, but in my opinion when you write something that is personal, you're saying "THIS IS ME." My book is about my battle with severe depression and I absolutely talk about my son Brendon, my daughter Lauren, and my husband Don. The beauty of writing something that is very personal is the ability to reveal, to expose and to not hide from anything. My son is 13, he is a hockey player, has many friends, and is a real boy's boy. I let him read the parts in my book where I use his name and I can honestly say, he didn't mind. (I actually think I saw a very small tear, though he'll probably mind me sharing that!) My advice would be to go with your gut but keep in mind that it's a great thing to write something that says "This is me, this is my life, this is my family and I'm not afraid to say it."

A: My book pretty much makes fun of my kids and I used their real names. I think it would get way too confusing to use other names...how about the back cover, dedication, promotions, interviews, etc.? I would maybe explain to the people in the book that this is YOUR journey and that everything is viewed from your point of view. I just read a book called *Straight Up and Dirty* about a woman's year in New York after her divorce...it was extremely personal and she said something similar in the introduction. Good luck!

A: If it is totally embarrassing and you feel ashamed of what you are discussing and feel it may have an impact on your family life or children's school life—why not change the names and write it as an alter ego, or say some of the things are based on factual events and the names have been changed.

A: If you are just a little scared of what might happen but didn't write anything that would put you in the "crazy family" category, or affect your children's social life, why not use the real names. Some thoughts:

    a) How are you going to promote it if you change your names?

    b) How are other families going to relate?

    b) People can gain valuable experience and inspiration by you revealing a life that you may not be proud of.

A: My book is VERY autobiographical as well and it could have a positive or negative effect on my career. I am really gambling with my book because I am revealing several things that I am not proud of. I am doing it to say to myself and the world—*THERE ARE NO SECRETS.* I am not the bearer of your secrets or mine. I want and need to grow and telling this story is going to make others and me grow. Truth is, I am already growing from writing and reading it. I really didn't want to change names but I did. I feel better not exposing other people who may feel offended or embarrassed.

A: Another option is penning the book under your maiden name and then just use your family's first names. It's up to you. The downside is that once you develop a following, it may confuse your audience when you use your married name. To combat that, you could us both your maiden and married name for work.

A: If you are concerned certain people will be hurt or offended, perhaps you can prepare them and show them the advance copies—so they are aware. And, if an individual has a problem with it, you can change their name, and a few details about them, so they are unrecognizable. You can talk about this upfront in the preface or intro, as in "Some names have been changed to protect the privacy of individuals I love and respect." Go with your heart.

A: My book is different, about infertility. I thought about using real names or not. I interviewed several people. I handled it by going to them and asking them their preference and then honored their wishes.

I wrote about myself, my husband, and my daughter, on a very personal level. Something that went into my thinking was how would my daughter feel if what I wrote in the book came back to her from somebody other than me. That is sort of the mantra I use when I counsel people regarding infertility and how and what to tell their kids. I think it may be applicable to your situation. You have to use your heart and your gut. Imagine how you would feel being interviewed by somebody about some of the personal, intimate aspects of your book and your comfort level in responding as yourself or as if you wrote about somebody else. Good luck.

The Sonogram — Seeing My Baby's Cover

NINA MARIE DURAN

When I first saw the cover I was amazed. I was flabbergasted. I was speechless. It really was almost like viewing a sonogram—seeing the shape of my book, seeing this outline, seeing what this is going to be. I showed Elijah, who is only 3 years-old and he said, "Mama, why am I there?" When he saw the "E" he recognized his name and was really excited, but he didn't really understand.

DEBORAH HURLEY

The instant that I saw the cover of my book for the first time, I knew it was absolutely perfect. I reviewed four different cover ideas and had to choose which one would convey best what my book was about. There was no doubt in my mind that the one I chose was the one that was meant to be. It spoke to me, it moved me and I felt it would speak to my readers. The reality of what was happening began to sink in and I actually gave myself permission to think of myself as an author. Those words sounded so cool to me "I am an author." It was unbelievable!

PAMELA JO LEO

When I got my final cover I thought, "This woman gets me. She knows what's in my heart." My publisher hired a professional illustrator to draw the hand images on my cover, but I wasn't happy with the first one. I worried, how can I tell her I don't like the child's hand? I knew I had to tell her, this is going to represent me to the whole world, it has to be what I need it to be. My publisher "Photoshopped" a new hand in, and it was perfect. Remember, it's important to have the inner power to stand up for your vision.

MALONDA RICHARD

I read somewhere that a great book cover can help book sales. My dream for the book cover was that it would give a reader a glimpse into the world they will experience when they read my book. I wanted people to look at the book and run to the register to purchase it.

The first draft of my cover was cute but the second draft was absolutely fabulous and I knew from the first moment I saw it that I had a winner. I immediately sent it out to family and friends. I was so happy to show my baby off. I truly believe that people are going to buy my book just because the book cover is hot. Looking at the cover gives me the inspiration to follow through on all of my goals for the book.

What makes a great book cover?

As a graphic designer with 20 years experience packaging books, for me a great cover goes back to the author's branding—the book is one visual part of a whole which is communicating a personality, an idea, a message. The cover needs to inform readers of the book's content and the author's style. The first place to start when planning your cover (or providing your cover ideas to your publisher) is a portfolio of your favorite covers, ones that have caught your eye in the past. Then search your book's genre on Amazon and see how the other authors reaching the same market are communicating their message on their covers.

Gather your ideas for colors, fonts and photography, along with cover samples that you love, and communicate with your editor or book designer directly. Know which design approach you would like to take— illustration, photography, abstract or graphic, collage, and whether or not *you* want to be on the cover.

A few cover design approaches...

Illustrated Covers

These covers (*and this book!*) were illustrated by Kelley Cunningham. www.kelleysart.com.

Thematic Photography

A powerful photograph which captures the book's theme.

Author Photo

The author in her element, with her family.

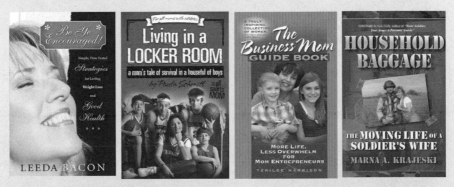

Abstract, Graphic or Collage

Here is my favorite cover to date. The author suggested "the back of my car with hilarious bumper-stickers," and we created this in Photoshop:

"What IS the matter with Mommy? Kelley Cunningham answers the age-old question in the only way she can...with a unique blend of humor and honesty."
~ Jennifer Niesslein & Stephanie Wilkinson, editors, *Brain, Child* magazine

What's the Matter with Mommy?

Rantings of a Reluctant Stay-at-Home Mother

PTA

Don't Follow Me Unless You Want To Wind Up At A Boring Soccer Game

I'd Rather Be Doing Anything Else

WINSTAR

WYMAN
NUTZ

New Jersey
MOM·B4U
Garden State

Yes, This Is My Minivan. No, I Won't Be A Driver on the Class Trip.

Just Shoot Me. I'm Listening To Radio Disney.

DECAF is for Weenies

If The Minivan's A' Rockin' The Kids Are A' Fightin'

I don't care who started it. I'm ending it.

My kid, What'shisname, is an honor student somewhere

I BRAKE FOR EGG CARTONS AND TOILET PAPER ROLLS

Don't Make Me Get The Wooden Spoon

Get In, Sit Down, Hold On and Shut Up!

No, we're NOT there yet, dammit!

CLINTON 2008
Put a Mother in Charge

Kelley Cunningham

Letting Go — Giving your Manuscript to the Publisher

CHRISTINE LOUISE HOHLBAUM

Releasing your manuscript into the big, bad world is much like sending your child off to college. You know the time is right, and yet you are filled with hesitation, concern, and trepidation. Was it the right thing to do? Is the book really ready for the whole world to experience? By the time I had learned about Nancy Cleary's Mom-Writers Publishing Cooperative, I had been through three failed attempts—I was ready to launch my book no matter what. The feeling was equivalent to having your child stay home longer than expected. No more community college, kiddo! It's time to fly!

MARNA KRAJESKI

The moment I sent the final manuscript to the publisher and released my baby—it felt terrible. As writers we know that works are never finished, they're just abandoned. And a writer with perfectionist tendencies like me will think that the manuscript is never just right, so it's pure torture to send it off.

MALONDA RICHARD

I finally finished the manuscript for my book last week and the experience was very similar to having a baby. The main difference was the birthing process for my book took over 5 years and my baby couldn't even wait until the delivery room!

Now that I have made this dream come true, I have a moment to acknowledge all of the amazing things that are happening to me. First, I feel a lot lighter and inspired to make more dreams come true. Second, I am receiving an amazing amount of support from family members and friends. I'm also receiving support from internet friends whom I've never met. Third, I am able to spend a little more quality time with my daughter.

I am excited about getting the first copies of my book and I know that the next year is going to be filled with more amazing things.

No wonder there are millions of people who may never have the chance to call themselves a published author. I, like so many people believed that half the battle of becoming an author was sitting down to record the ideas and thoughts that make up a book. But in my experience writing is only one-third of the journey. Don't get me wrong, completing a manuscript that can be read by people other than your relatives or closest friends is an amazing feat in itself.

I decided to print my pregnancy journals because I truly believe that they can be a catalyst for amazing things. Writing a book comprised of journals has been as challenging as writing from a blank page. I have probably edited my manuscript over 60 times and I still have more edits before the book goes to print.

I am learning valuable lessons and recognizing the major accomplishment that I have already achieved. In a few weeks, I will be a bonafide, published author and I will have made my own dream come true. I will be a third of the way on my journey to becoming a successful author.

CAROLINE POSER

Sometimes I wonder why should anyone care about what I have to say. Then I remember what one of my friends told me once—that everyone has a story to tell, but not everyone bothers to tell it. Initial feedback from my peers has been positive. I feel compelled to publish it and I feel compelled to keep writing.

I have noticed that I am having a tough time finalizing the manuscript. Part of it is sheer lack of time; often I'm only able to spend 15 minutes here and there on the book. Or I sit down and look at it in the evening but am physically exhausted. I have started to wonder, though, if I am torturing the copy because I am afraid for some reason to "let it go." It's like being at the end of your pregnancy and really wanting to have that baby, yet not wanting to because you know your life will never be the same again.

I printed it out for a third time to make yet another round of edits. The professional editor I contacted did not get back to me, so I started reading it out loud to the baby, because he is the only one who listens to me. I know I'll be more likely to catch anything hinky if I hear it out loud.

ALANA MORALES

I am having a problem with getting this book done. There are several things that lead to this horrible fact. One, I work full time from home, which I don't recommend to anyone who wants to keep their sanity intact and write a book.

Two, I'm indecisive and feel like I need more direction with it. I know that I want to say certain things, but what if I'm not saying them the right way?

Three, what if it sucks? I mean, I see these other people who are coming out with books similar to mine and it pisses me off. Then I think —what if mine doesn't even compare to theirs, much less surpass it? What if no one besides my family reads it?

I have to finish it—I'm under contract. But it is *so* much harder than I thought it would be. I didn't expect it to be easy. I just thought it would somehow come together easier. Maybe I thought that little magical book fairies would spring out of my computer, offering me guidance on how to organize my book. Then again, maybe I just need to get more sleep.

JULIE WATSON SMITH

Truth be told, I suffered a literary kind of post-partum baby blues. I felt emptiness inside when I sent off my manuscript. The manuscript had consumed so much of my life—collecting diaries, editing, writing. What was I going to do now that "my baby" has flown the coop? Little did I know that book toddlerhood would be even more time-consuming!

DEBORAH HURLEY

I definitely feel like a mother who is very ready to give birth. I have post-it notes all over, I have lists reminding me to do some final things, I am wrapping holiday gifts, cleaning out closets, reorganizing shelves and believe it or not I even have our Christmas cards made out. I am due in December and boy oh boy am I ready! I have spent the past few weeks gathering up my endorsements, finding more mistakes in my book, contacting local newspapers, planning my book launch party and going into book stores. I'm exhausted! I sit back sometimes and reflect on the past year and I can't believe how far I've come. I remember the very first email I sent Nancy, where I sounded desperate, defeated and hopeless. It's amazing how things can completely turn around in one year's time. I am more confident than I have ever been. Wish me luck on my delivery... I'm sure you will hear the screams of sweet relief coming from Eastern Long Island!

SAMANTHA GIANULIS

Baby was sleeping, kids were at school, I was typing away on my laptop when I reached the last edit on the last page. No more scribbled notes in red ultra fine point Sharpie. No more keeping *this* baby under wraps from the world. I reluctantly clicked "compose," and wrote an email to Nancy stating, "I'm delivering today!" I faced my dreams with a little fear. The coffee maker beeped and turned off. I hit "send."

CHRISTIE GLASCOE CROWDER

Yesterday afternoon I sent my manuscript to Wyatt-MacKenzie. I'd had a hectic day, and the day before was worse. The day before was when I received the final edits and I gave my book its last once-over. I didn't eat the whole day and didn't realize it until my phone and computer alerted me that it was time to pick up my daughter Kennedy from school.

The next day was really full too and I wanted to get the manuscript printed out so I could send it while I was out. I put extra paper in the printer. I took the toner cartridge out and gave it a good shake so it wouldn't fade on me. File. Print. I felt like I was going up the hill to the first drop on the Superman rollercoaster at Six Flags Great America as each page rolled out of the printer. With shaky hands I stacked the pages neatly and fastened them with a binder clip. I put it in my brief case between my journal/to-do list notebook and my client's file. I somehow felt it would be safer tucked between these two other coveted collections of information concerning my entire life. I was protective of it all morning—none of my normal flinging my bag around and leaving it unattended at my client's office. I even had a fleeting thought of securing it in the seat belt in case I slammed on the brakes in always unpredictable Atlanta traffic, so it wouldn't fly out of my bag into the footwell of my front seat.

"I need to send a package cheap and quick," I said to the UPS Store clerk. "The quickest and cheapest is 2-day priority," he said. "I'll take it." I thought seriously about spending the extra money for 1-day but one more day of anxiety-ridden suspense would not completely kill me. Watching my first manuscript disappear into the envelope turned me green. My stomach jumped into my throat and my head began to swim. "Wait," I thought. "I'm not finished. I forgot this...I forgot that... I didn't mention this...I'm not ready." Too late...it's sealed. "Have a good day, ma'am." Have a good day? You are sending my baby to Deadwood, Oregon by herself! I practically walked backwards out the door watching the clerk's every move. Another fleeting thought... canceling the delivery and getting on a plane myself. That way I can hand deliver it and stand over Nancy's shoulder while she reads it and explain my reasons for every sentence. Okay, I need to get a grip.

As the door shut behind me and I headed to my car, a surprising sense of relief and satisfaction wafted over me. I was done. I completed my very first manuscript and it was off to be published. Wow! I got in my car and dialed Nancy. I really wanted her to pick up. In a quivering voice, I left her a message that I had sent her the manuscript. "I hope it doesn't suck," I said. Why did I say that? It just came out. Fear and anxiety rushed back as if a dam had burst. Thoughts of actually having to sell this book filled my head and so did self-doubt.

Nancy apparently got my message because the next morning there was a posting on our MWPC chat board about the fear and anxiety of sending your manuscript to the publisher. She said exactly what I needed to hear. I'm feeling a little better now...well except for the regret of saying "I hope my book doesn't suck."

What's an ARC?

ARC stands for "Advance Reading Copy" or "Advance Review Copy." It was once referred to as a "galley" when printers would run the interior pages and bind them with a plain paper cover. These days we simply do digital printing of these pre-pub proofs. It is a crucial step of the publishing and promotion process.

What are the ARCs used for?

- Gathering early endorsements for the book—to print in marketing materials and on the back cover

- Pitching to print magazines with long turnaround times, six or more months before the book comes out

- Submission to major reviewers 4-5 months before the pub date (*See Resources.*)

What goes in the **Advance Review Package**
Printed and bound ARC
Experts do not want a box of loose laser prints, or even single-side printed and spiral bound manuscripts—they want it perfect-bound and typeset with an image of the cover on the front and all of the publishing details including: title, subtitle, ISBN, page count, price, format (hardcover or paperback), LCCN, distributor, bisac categories (Google "BISAC SUBJECT HEADINGS"), and contact info.
Cover Letter
Press Release
An all-inclusive release dated into the future to provide the tone of future media presentations
Sell Sheet
One-page flyer with book info plus headline, description, testimonials, cover, author bio, author photo and contact info.

Example of an ARC package for a pre-pub review is on the following pages.

Who do the ARC packages go to? *See Chapter 3 Tech Talk.*

Cover of ARC

Bound ARC

Press Release

FOR RELEASE NOVEMBER 1, 2006

Wyatt-MacKenzie Releases Much-Anticipated Book "What's The Matter With Mommy?" by Popular Syndicated Humor Writer Kelley Cunningham

Deadwood, OR. (PR.Web) November 1, 2006 – Fans have been clamoring their keyboards since Kelley Cunningham launched her popular online column, "What's the Matter With Mommy? ... humorous rants on some of the absurdities of modern motherhood"

"Fans begged me to wrangle my column into book form," admits veteran humor writer Kelley Cunningham. "Some of them actually cried. It was embarrassing." To avoid the pitfalls of columnist turned lukewarm short story collector, Cunningham carefully crafted her collection to include the best of the best. "What's The Matter With Mommy: Rantings of a Reluctant Stay-at-Home Mom", to be released November 30, is the result.

"Brutally and hysterically honest, Kelley says what many moms stifle," says publisher at Wyatt-MacKenzie, Nancy Cleary, who is thrilled to add "What's The Matter With Mommy" to their roster of talented mom authors. This independent press has been publishing moms since 1999. Cunningham, along with 21 other mom authors, are members of the Mom-Writers Publishing Co-Op a group that shares publicity, cross promotion, and profits.

Cunningham's work has appeared in *The Funny Times*, *Mothering Magazine*, and *Brain, Child* magazine. Her monthly column "What's The Matter With Mommy?" was syndicated on the popular webzines imperfectparent.com and Quirkee.com. Kelley is also an award-winning fine artist and an illustrator of children's books, magazine covers and articles, and book covers for leading publishers. She was an art director for ten years at a number of New York advertising agencies and currently serves as art director at a major children's magazine.

"What's the Matter with Mommy? Rantings of a Reluctant Stay-at-Home Mom" (Wyatt-MacKenzie, Nov. 30, 2006) by Kelley Cunningham, ISBN: 1-932279-29-6 168 Pages, 5.25 x 8.25, $14.50 Trade Paperback. Distributed by CDS Books/Perseus, available at your favorite bookstore.

Contact Information:
For author interviews: Kelley Cunningham, kelley@kelleysart.com
Publicity contact: Nancy Cleary, nancy@wymacpublishing.com
Wyatt-MacKenzie Publishing
Deadwood, OR. 541-964-3314
http://www.WyMacPublishing.com

What s the Matter with Mommy? Rantings of a Reluctant Stay-at-Home Mom
by Kelley Cunningham

ISBN: 1-932279-29-6, ISBN-13: 978-1-932279-29-0
Pub Date: NOV. 30, 2006
168 Pages, 5.25 x 8.25
$14.50 Trade Paperback
HUMOR/Family
FAMILY & RELATIONSHIPS/Parenting/Motherhood

DISTRIBUTED BY:
CDS BOOKS/PERSEUS BOOKS, NY
1-800-343-4499

Kelley Cunningham is a syndicated humor writer and a contributor to *The Funny Times*, *Mothering* and *Brain, Child* magazines. Her monthly column, on which *What s The Matter With Mommy?* is based, is syndicated on the popular webzines www.imperfectparent.com and Quirkee.com. Kelley is also an award-winning fine artist and an illustrator of children s books, magazine covers and articles, and book covers for leading publishers. She was an art director for ten years at a number of New York advertising agencies and currently serves as art director at a major children s magazine.

For author interviews: **kelley@kelleysart.com**

"Brutally and hysterically honest, Kelley says what many moms stifle."

This anthology of essays from the author s monthly column *"What's the Matter With Mommy? ... humorous rants on some of the absurdities of modern motherhood"* received an extraordinary amount of fan mail soliciting it in book form. Kelley s fans are lining up to purchase this funny book by their hero.

MARKETING HIGHLIGHTS:
· Excerpt Mom-Writers Literary Magazine
· Internet Radio Tour
· Internet mom-author blog tour
· PA, NJ, NY Book Tour

· To be featured on over 2 dozen mom-centric web sites reaching a total audience of 5 million in Fall 06

PUBLICITY CONTACT:
Nancy Cleary
Tel: 541-964-3314
nancy@wymacpublishing.com

PENDING
· 3 Major Women s print magazines considering for Holiday Issues
· Local PA, NJ, NY Newspapers will feature book and author events
· Local PA, NJ, NY TV

· Endorsements pending from high-profile authors and celebrity personalities

Wyatt-MacKenzie Publishing, Inc.
DEADWOOD, OREGON
www.WyMacPublishing.com

Sell Sheet

Pitch Letter

Lifestyles Forecasts
Publisher's Weekly
360 Park Ave South, 13th floor
New York, NY 10010-1710

August 1, 2006

Dear Editor,

Thank you for considering this title for a possible mention in Forecasts.

A recent article in The *New York Times*, "Sorry, Motherhood is Boring", pointed to the backlash of excessive child-centeredness and the resentment mothers feel for the mundane tasks they must perform. **What's The Matter With Mommy? Rantings of a Reluctant Stay-at-Home Mom** brings the reader – mom, dad, or other – on a hysterical ride through the absurdity with an uncensored view on the new implied "rules" for parenthood.

"If You Don't Finish Your Kelp, You Can't Have any Acidophilus" is a plea to save us all from overly critical organic moms who can afford to pay twice the price while chanting "But if you buy organic it s better for the planet" as they pull out of the Whole Foods parking lot in their Yukon Denalis. "A New and Improved *Zagats For Parents*" provides not-so-family-friendly reviews. "The Envelope, Please" offers the Mommy Awards – from "The Sylvia Plath Award" for extreme mother martyrdom to the "Mea Maxima Culpa" for outstanding achievement in bad mothering and the "Baby Bop Award" to the kiddie show characters you just want to fucking strangle.

WARNING: The language in **What's The Matter With Mommy?** is not appropriate for the kids – so keep this book with the healthy snacks and chapter books (where they'll never find it).

Enclosed you will find two copies of the galley, a press release, and info sheet. Thank you for your time – if you're a parent, I bet you ll have to hide your laughter.

Warm regards,
Nancy Cleary
Publicity

For further queries, please contact the publicity dept., Nancy Cleary, Tel: 541-964-3314
nancy@wymacpublishing.com

What's a **pitch?**

Before sending the ARC packages you must ask if your intended recipient wants it! This involves a pitch—wrapping your message and request into something that is beneficial to the recipient, or at least proves their action will have a positive affect on a market segment which is near and dear to their heart.

You will learn more about Pitching in Part Two.

Example of author's pitch letter for cover blurb (once some initial contact has been made)

Christine Louise Hohlbaum • Reichertshausener Str. 4a • 85307 Paunzhausen, Germany • Tel: 011 49 8444 919270
Email: christine@diaryofamother.com • www.SAHMIAM.net

Jack Canfield
P.O. Box XXX
City, State, Zip
USA

February 9, 2005

Dear Mr. Canfield,

Thank you for your interest in **SAHM I Am: Tales of a Stay-at-Home Mom in Europe** (Wyatt-MacKenzie Publishing, May 2005) for a possible endorsement.

Stay-at-home moms require a great deal of support. **SAHM I Am** offers moms an outlet by letting them know we are all in this together—through the laughter and the tears. It is like an Oprah talk show in book form, allowing readers to feel understood through the traumatic and thought-provoking experiences I describe.

Cynthia Brian, co-author of the *New York Times* best-selling book **Chicken Soup for the Gardener's Soul** who also wrote the foreword to **SAHM I Am**, said it best: "Christine is the type of person you want in your circle of friends. She finds the beauty and the laughter in the simplest situations. She sees the world through the eyes of her children."

Enclosed you will find my latest press release and bio for your convenience.

I look forward to hearing your thoughts.

Warm regards,

Christine Louise Hohlbaum
Author of **Diary of a Mother: Parenting Stories and Other Stuff** (2003)
SAHM I Am: Tales of a Stay-at-Home Mom in Europe (May 2005)

For further queries, please contact the publisher, Nancy Cleary, Wyatt-MacKenzie Publishing, 15115 Highway 36, Deadwood, OR 97430-9700, nancy@wymacpublishing.com, Tel: 541-964-3314, Fax: 541-964-3315

The complete ARC package sent with cover letter.

Receiving...then Sending Out the ARCs

SAMANTHA GIANULIS

A-R-C Spells Happy Me! My daughter Zoë still sits in her Care Bears pajamas on the couch, the baby is taking a nap, and it is past ten o'clock. It is a reasonable time for a package to be on the front porch. I didn't hear the loud engine of the UPS truck or the sliding metal door of the FedEx van, but the books could be there, nonetheless. How obsessive-compulsive is it to peek through the door and see if my dream has been delivered? Hell, I don't care, I've gotta look. Two cardboard boxes on the front porch. One sits on top of the other.

"ZOE! Come to the front door, hurry!" She picks up the excitement in my voice, and her four year-old frame comes tearing around the corner. Damn, I hope I didn't wake up the baby.

"What Mama?" she asks. "My ARCs are here." I bend down to look in her sable eyes. Zoë puts her hands over her mouth, jumps up and down and squeals, "This is so exciting, oh my gosh!" I am so happy I get to share this moment with an already exuberant spirit. My son may well have said, "That's cool, Mom." with a shrug.

Zoë runs and gets the scissors. "No, the big ones!" I say after she hands me her toddler scissors from the craft store. She's excited she gets to use the big guns on a big box. Together, we cut through the clear tape with black scuffs, and behold—the manifestation of a promise I made myself when I quit my last official job.

Thirty advanced reading copies of my book, *Little Grapes on the Vine...Mommy Musings on Food & Family*, due out next April. It's unreal! I drove a copy of my ARC to my aunt's, and my mom's (at every red light I opened it up and read until someone honked at me to go). Then showed my girlfriends at my son's school. The rest of the copies are reserved for the media—it sounds so official, press releases, book signings, newspapers, magazines...here we go!

Until now, I have been intimidated by such things. Holding my advance copy in my hands I am infused with energy and purpose—my work is not over, but I have a shiny ARC to hold as I find the right words to say.

The laundry remains unfolded. The dishes remain unwashed. I am back on the couch with my daughter reading my book—and I am focused. I am ecstatic! I did what I said I was going to do many years ago. So, there's that. And a whole lot more. It's *me* in that book. It's me and my kitchen and my thought process and all my neuroses!

CHRISTIE GLASCOE CROWDER

Happy Birthday to Me! My 34th birthday was a couple of weeks ago and aside from the lovely charm bracelet my husband gave me, I got the best birthday present...the bound advance review copies of my book! No, not the real book but the copies you send out for the media to read and write reviews (if they choose to.) Granted, not completely as exciting as getting the real thing, but for a first time author...very, very close. If I was still in denial about actually publishing a book, receiving these "mock ups" catapulted me into reality. I was beaming from ear to ear. For me, it might as well have been the real book. Imagine how I will feel when the real ones do arrive. It will be like the Publishers Clearing House truck pulling up. This is just one of the many milestones we authors cherish in this process. Every little step brings us closer to our dreams fulfilled.

CAROLINE POSER

When the ARCs came, I didn't even have a list of people who I wanted to contact. I managed to get the bulk of my reviews in one month's time. It was a miracle.

I started requesting endorsements when I had the ARCs in hand. Talk about behind the eight ball! That's what happens with three kids and a full time job. But I think it will be okay. I have about three and a half more weeks and have asked a few more people as of yesterday.

One of my reviewers said "No." She said that the book lacked substance and that it read like a diary. She realized that this was probably my intention, but she couldn't endorse it. I understood intellectually what she said; her books are as detailed as Ph.D. theses, because she *is* a Ph.D. I suppose I am in a totally different genre than she is. Maybe I was wrong to ask her. My feelings were a little hurt at first, but when I received the blurb for my cover from Mark Victor Hansen I quickly forgot the pain! And then Julie Tilsner, author and contributing editor of *Parenting* magazine, *and* Jane Swift, the former Governor of Massachusetts, both sent great advance reviews! I worked hard to get those in a short time and this is where my sales experience paid off. I had plenty to put on my back cover and inside pages.

IRIS WAICHLER

I vividly remember when my publisher, Nancy, asked me who was on my wish list of people to endorse my book, *Riding the Infertility Roller Coaster*. I was really caught off guard by that question. I had not even considered it. Why would somebody who didn't know me consider endorsing my book? The person who came to mind immediately was Christiane Northrup, MD. I had been following her work for years. She was a leading authority on women's health and was that rare doctor who was also a patient advocate. I wrote her a letter explaining my personal battle with infertility and my wish to help as many people as I could who were engaged in this struggle. I really didn't expect any kind of response. To my utter surprise and delight I received a letter from her saying she would be happy to help and she did indeed endorse my book!

When I got her letter I had a flashback to 1976, when I wrote a letter to Katharine Hepburn. I was a huge fan of hers. I was inspired to write her a letter thanking her for her work advancing the role of women in films. I also told her how much I enjoyed her interview with Dick Cavett where she definitely stole the show. My only hope was that she would receive the letter. Imagine my amazement when on my birthday I got a letter on the personal stationery of Katharine Houghton Hepburn thanking me for "your sweet note" and sharing, "how happy it made me."

I learned a valuable lesson from both of these great women—don't be afraid to contact people you feel may be out of reach to help with your book, project, and/or cause. Speak to them honestly and from your heart.

I don't want to give the impression that I have not failed in my attempts to get endorsements. I was turned down by Brenda Strong, voice of *Desperate Housewives*, Naomi Wolf, the feminist author, and others. If you have the courage to contact people sometimes you may be happily surprised.

PAMELA JO LEO

I just had to share my most exciting news! The one endorsement I wanted MOST of all for *Connection Parenting*, was from Joseph Chilton Pearce, author of *Magical Child*. I sent him my CD, thinking getting an endorsement for the CD would be a great start to getting one for the book. When I didn't hear back from him I followed up and it turns out he didn't think he got the CD, but his exact email words were: "I am happy to endorse anything you care to say, write or do." WOOO HOOO, I am doing the happy dance tonight!

Three of my dreams for this book are: 1) an endorsement from Joseph Chilton Pearce; 2) to have it translated into other languages; 3) to have it on *Oprah*. So far we have Joseph, a Spanish version in progress, foreign rights sales to Korea, Russia, Japan and Isreal in the works, and will be at the International Publishers Alliance Booth at the 2007 BEA in NYC. *Oprah...?* You were right Nancy, the Universe is saying YES, YES, YES!

DEBORAH HURLEY

On September 24th 2007, I received an email from London that had me literally floating on air. It all began with a simple Google search on "Depression." There was one particular article that left an impression on me, written by Lewis Wolpert, and I decided to research more about him. I was impressed to find that Dr. Wolpert is a Professor of Biology at the University College in London, the author of ten books, and a Fellow of the Royal Society of Literature. His book *Malignant Sadness* was the basis for three television programs in London called "A Living Hell;" he has presented science on both radio and television for five years; and he himself has suffered with severe depression.

The more I read, the more intrigued I became, and the more I realized that although he is a literary and scientific expert, his suffering and pain was as real and as horrific as mine. I eagerly looked up the University College in London and quickly found my way to The Department of Anatomy and found Dr. Wolpert's email address. I composed a short, but informative, email asking if I could send an ARC. Within an hour there was a reply in my mailbox and with my heart pounding out of my chest I opened it. The reply was from London and it read: "Please send, Lewis"

On October 9th 2006, I received my third email from London. This was the one I had been waiting for. As I lay next to my husband in bed, we eagerly opened the email and he read it to me aloud. It said: "Have read your book: very moving and hope you are doing well. If you want a quote, this may be OK: "A most moving account of a terrible depression and a recovery." Regards, Lewis.

I closed my eyes and thought about who I was and what I had just done. At that moment I couldn't help but reflect upon the many years I had struggled to become whole inside. That particular email evoked emotions in me that will never be forgotten. My eyes welled with up with tears as I realized that my voice had been heard. It absolutely blew my mind to think that me—a homemaker, a stay-at-home mom, an average everyday woman who had suffered with depression for so long—was receiving emails from Dr. Lewis Wolpert in London. I couldn't believe that one simple Google search had been transformed into an endorsement for my book from someone like Wolpert. I remained in bed for an hour with my comforter pulled right up to my chin. I read his email over and over aloud. Dr. Wolpert would never know how his one little email had changed my world, and how his acknowledgement of me and my work had helped me to believe in myself. I had spent so many years thinking that I wasn't capable, that I couldn't and that I wouldn't but there I was, a 37 year-old woman in Long Island, snuggled beneath her covers, who wanted to, who could, and who actually did.

DEBORAH HURLEY

I had a really bad case of the "What ifs." What if my book really stunk? What if I was the only one who thought that it was any good? What if I couldn't handle a bad review? What if I got negative feedback? What if nobody bought it? I felt like such a fraud. Who was I, and what made me worthy of becoming an author? I was not a doctor and I had no formal schooling in my book's topic. I had experience but was my experience enough to make me an expert? Did I need to be an expert on what I had written? Who says that I did? Where was that rule? I was a stay-at-home mother and now I was becoming an author. That blew my mind. I needed reassurance that my book would be well received. Although I was ready to show the world what I had to offer, I felt myself becoming needy.

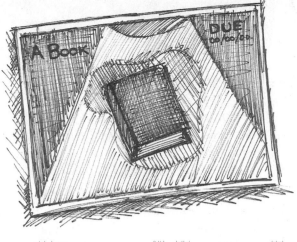

CHAPTER 3

Pre-Natal Care

Book Midwifery

*J*UST AS WE TOOK CARE OF OURSELVES AND prepared when we were pregnant—regular check-ups to see the sonograms, child-birth classes to learn how to breathe, and a "birth plan" so the hospital stay and delivery were everything we hoped—the pre-publication process requires just as much preparation, and comes with an equal dose of anxiety and fear. Co-op members share their pre-natal marketing plans...as well as their cravings, weight gain, and morning sickness!

Why, like babies, do books need 9-month birthing plans? And do authors need to hire a professional PR agent? Tech Talk has the answers.

"Depending on the time of day, the publishing process has created additional cravings for coffee, chocolate and wine."

IN THIS CHAPTER

Morning sickness • Weight Gain • Cravings

Tech Talk
What's a **"Publication Date"**?
The Nine-Month Book Birthing Plan

Our Marketing Plans

Tech Tips — *To Hire a Professional PR Agent, Or Not?*

Cravings, Bad Dreams and Pain-Killers

CHRISTIE GLASCOE CROWDER

How funny is this—I am pregnant with my second child and my book will be born roughly one month before the baby! All of the nausea and sleepless nights and anxiety I thought were book related (maybe they were), I can now blame on my growing fetus. When I finished my book, I actually thought I could relax for a while before getting on the publicity trail, but then I realized that advance review copies would have to be sent out in about 1-2 months and I about passed out. I mean...I really thought writing the book was the hard part.

ALANA MORALES

I need an epidural—or at the very least a few martinis.

JULIE WATSON SMITH

Depending on the time of day, the publishing process has created additional cravings for coffee, chocolate and wine. As much as I prefer to have most pain dulled, I now appreciate following the saying "no pain, no gain" during the pre-pub process. Had I not experienced both the ups and downs of delivering my book, I wouldn't have gained the added insight, focus and direction to carry out both my personal and professional desires.

SAMANTHA GIANULIS

My body is acting like it is pregnant. I am not making this up. I am two and a half weeks late with the added bonus of cramps and I've been craving soup and roasted chicken. I have gained three pounds and I have regressed back to finishing the food on the kids' plates. Stress equals hunger for me.

I have a glass of wine to calm me down while I make dinner. This backfires, and instead gets my creative juices flowing like a ripe Meyer lemon. I furiously scribble marketing plans in the composition book I keep by my stove.

KATHRYN MAHONEY

When it comes to talking about my book or selling it, I would have loved an epidural and a strong shot of tequila wouldn't hurt either. Have I been nauseous in the mornings? Oh man, that's an understatement; the first six months were daunting. I didn't quite know what I was doing, but through the help of my publisher and the grace of God, I seemed to make it through.

CHRISTINE LOUISE HOHLBAUM

It must be the mid-life spread because in the last three years, I have become elongated sideways. It's nothing noticeable to the casual viewer, but I feel it. Every summer my clothes feel a bit snugger and my butt fills more of the mirror. It must be that I'm writing yet another book. Oh my goodness, I have book butt!

DEBORAH HURLEY

I had completely lost my appetite and I simply could not sleep. I continuously woke up all night long pinching myself and wondering if it was actually true. I wanted to become an author for so long and now that it was going to happen, it felt surreal. I was afraid to tell people because I thought that once I did, I would wake up from my dream.

NINA MARIE DURAN

Oh my gosh, I was having bad dreams that the cover was not Elijah but some other kid. Dreams taunted me. I'd be freaking out at 2:00 am. So much emailing. Being in contact with the local newspapers. Every morning opening my email I'd get morning sickness—I'd feel butterflies and wonder, am I going to get a response? Some mornings were great, someone would want to interview me. But there were other mornings.... The anticipation of opening the emails was my morning sickness.

PAULA SCHMITT

At this point I feel awesome! I wake in the morning looking forward to the day and accomplishing my goals. I even went as far as hiring a PR agent to help me. With the help of my agent I have a birth plan for the book—wow, there is so much PR involved that I am happy to have help. My agent and I have planned to send out press releases and galleys to several radio, newspaper, magazine and television media. I also set up several book events.

IRIS WAICHLER

I did have many nights where I couldn't sleep and I lay awake thinking about new ways I might get publicity, or get reviewed. I must confess that I find myself looking at Amazon.com regularly to see if there are new reviews or my sales figures have risen. My ongoing interest in this has surprised me. I was asked to do a radio program and I stayed awake all night thinking about what I would say.

CAROLINE POSER

I'm exhausted. For the past week I have fallen asleep on the couch with my laptop on my lap every night

MALONDA RICHARD

I feel honored to be able to give birth to my book but I also feel guilty because I know that there are so many other writers out there who may never have the opportunity to give birth to their babies.

JENNIFER KALITA

I had a bit of queasiness thinking about actually putting my ideas into book form. Although I write columns, articles, press releases and web copy every week, the idea of writing a "book" was a bit overwhelming (and nauseating) to me. My dear friend and editor, Felicia Barlow, reframed the challenge for me, and encouraged me to write ten articles based on my chapter titles. So that's what I did, and four days later I turned around to find that I had actually written a book. No weight gain, as once I started writing my articles I couldn't stop writing and subsisted on whatever plates of food my husband so lovingly put on my desk.

The other pregnancy symptom I experienced was "nesting." Before I write, I need to have files organized, clutter dealt with, and closets organized. It may be a form of procrastination, but I need to have everything well organized before I can tap into the creative space I need to write well. I can write if the nesting hasn't occurred, but I don't write as well.

What is the "Publication Date"?

I've seen so many people define this one wrong, or not clearly state the importance of this date.

The Book industry has the same timelines as the Fashion Industry—if it's summer, there are winter fashions on the runway, and winter catalogs on the way to book buyers. If it's fall, expect to see what's coming next spring.

Why should you know this schedule? Book buyers will be ordering books from distributors 6 to 7 months ahead of the pub date, and, they will base their orders on the proposed media which will coincide with this date.

The Dream of Being on the Bookstore Shelf — Shattered

The reason it is so important to time all of your media to hit during the publication month is because bookstores will *only* keep those books that buyers ordered (6 7 months ago) on the shelf for 90 days. After only two months have passed, the bookstore owner will decide whether to pay for the books that have not sold, or return them for a full credit (and not have to pay the distributor, or publisher's bill—in fact, the publisher pays the shipping and a returns fee.)

Which books STAY on the bookstore shelf? As you can imagine, with almost 200,000 books published this year, even the 5% which qualify for major bookstore distribution can't all fit on the shelves. They only have room for long-selling classics, high-profile and celebrity authors, and books with $100,000+ marketing budgets. The rest are returned. Stores can always reorder at a later date.

While the dream many writers hold is to "have my book in the bookstores"—the reality is that it will only be there a few months, IF it makes it there at all. So the more planning ahead of time, the better!

Nine-Month Book Birthing Plan

6 - 7 Months until Publication Date

Create list of reviewers in the industry, potential endorsers, celebrities, experts, leaders in the field – who you will ask if they'd like to review an Advance Reading Copy, or perhaps write a foreword, or an introduction, or provide an endorsement.

Send pitches for print magazines reaching your target market for excerpts, reviews, or feature stories. You should be familiar with the magazine and pitch according to their editorial calendar. For regular columns, a minimum of 6 months ahead of the target month is usual for most monthlies; weeklies will have a slightly shorter lead time.

4 - 5 Months until Publication Date

Send ARCs to major reviewers: *Publishers Weekly, Library Journal, Kirkus, ALA Booklist, Foreword Magazine*, and major newspaper and magazine book review sections.

- Follow-up on reviews, endorsements and front matter contributors.
- Follow-up with print magazine pitch contacts.
- Prepare national TV pitches, gather contacts for your target shows. You should be familiar with the news or talk show format you want to pitch and have unique, relevant angles.

3 - 4 Months until Publication Date

Gather reporter contacts for local newspapers and TV news and entertainment shows.

- Make TV pitches to local, small venues
- Plan Events / Other Book Launch Events
    Consider hosting an event at a retail store, a restaurant, a children's play center, a church, or a community center.
    Make invitations and posters, etc.
- Pitch Radio Interviews – local terrestrial (AM/FM), internet podcasts, and then national and satellite radio.

Your goal is to first do well with the local media, archive the clips, and then parlay this success in your national pitches.

2-3 Months until Publication Date

- Finalize Book Release Events—if you are doing a bookstore tour, call the stores now to be sure your books will be stocked, suggest collaborative event promotions (like local TV!) If you are having your launch and signing party outside of bookstores your invitations should be ready to print and mail.
- Plan Blog Tour — ask everyone in your network to read an advance review copy of your book and review it on their blog
- Pitch Radio venues

Send copies of final book to all contributors, endorsers, and others in your network. Ask them to help build the buzz for the release next month.

1 Month until Publication Date

Announce any upcoming media successes (magazines, papers, radio, TV) everywhere—on your site, your blog, in your newsletter, to everyone you have pitched along the way and in a press release posted on PRWeb.com two weeks before publication.

- Blog & Radio Tour in progress this month and next
- Local TV Appearances
- Make National TV pitches with clips

Publication Month

- Book Release Events
- National TV Appearances
- Print Magazines hit stands (which were pitched 6 months ago)

1 Month after Publication Date

- Parlay any print magazine, newspaper, blog or TV to get more media

2 Months after Publication Date

Plan a Press Release Campaign — check Chases.com for holidays and events you can wrap around your book and its market. Continue to watch trends and current news stories for relevant ideas and angles to pitch.

Our Marketing Plans

I asked the co-op members to share their marketing plans and talk about one of their biggest concerns—whether or not to hire a PR agent.

JULIE WATSON SMITH

I did not hire a PR agent in the beginning thinking I could do it myself. I did a fairly decent job on the grassroots and local community level. However, I am now interviewing PR agents to take me further with increased national and international coverage.

I had the sketch of a birth plan, but once that first heavy contraction hit, it all went out the window. In other words, book marketing plans should evolve with what is going on in both your life and the world. I was so consumed with everything else that I forgot to revisit my sketched plan.

PAULA SCHMITT

I hired a PR agent to help promote me and my book. There is so much PR involved that I was happy to have help. My agent sent press releases and galleys to her contacts in radio, newspaper, magazine and television media, and we had a ton of success.

IRIS WAICHLER

I do not have a PR agent. I currently have five readings/signings scheduled at my local bookstores and am cultivating some contacts out of state. As the date for my book release grows closer I am anxious about how it will be received and reviewed. Focusing on the marketing piece to show the world "my baby" is the most difficult part for me.

There will also be an article in *Parent* Magazine and I have written an article to be syndicated, excerpting a chapter of my book and plugging it at the end. I hope to be speaking at a conference in May with my book title as the topic.

I have sent letters or ARCs to everybody from Oprah to the *New York Times* and all of the local TV, newspaper, and radio talk shows. I have sent it to everyone I know who does book reviews including *The American Library Association*, *Time*, and *Newsweek* magazines.

I did have a birth plan put together beginning 6 months from when my book would be published. I documented everything I did, and the response. I contacted people on a weekly basis and researched places where the population I was targeting would be looking. I worked with Nancy on putting together a sell sheet, website, and press release, and in finding an illustrator, indexer, editor and proofreader. I networked as much as I possibly could. I also contacted people regarding endorsements.

This process would have been painful without the help and support of the members of the co-op. I would not have known where to go to do many of the things outlined above without their input.

ALANA MORALES

I desperately wanted to hire a PR agent, but at several thousand dollars a month it was just not an option. So I did what I normally do, and turned to books. I found several good book promotion books—my favorite is *The Frugal Book Promoter*. I also found a bunch of helpful websites. I feel confident in my ability to do most of the stuff, but the time will be the biggest issue for me.

CHRISTINE LOUISE HOHLBAUM

Living in Europe and promoting in the U.S. has been challenging. Nonetheless, I've managed to develop relationships with many media members through email, networking, interviews, and phone calls. Occasionally, I have to get up at 3 am to conduct an evening interview on the West Coast, but who wouldn't do that for her baby, huh?

The good news is—I have developed a vast network of media and PR contacts. I've even been hired by other PR agencies to do writing for their clients. It is gratifying to know a second career has come of my writing.

With my first book, I didn't have a clue how important a marketing plan was. By the time the second book came around I had the know-how, and the contacts, to put together a strong campaign.

JENNIFER KALITA

As a national consultant and speaker, I devote a great deal of time to maintaining media momentum in general, so my regular interviews really paid off when the book came out. People don't buy books, they buy people, so I am constantly speaking and marketing my book through my e-zine, seminars and various engagements. Many people rely on their publishers to create buzz around the book, but the truth is that it is up to the author to promote her own book if she wants to boost sales and speaking engagement revenue around her book.

LEEDA BACON

Planning for the anticipated bundle of joy is very challenging. There's a constant feeling that you may have forgotten something crucial, since this is your first. Have you done everything possible to keep the baby happy? You find that everything you do, everything you say and every waking moment is focused on the baby. It is much the same with a book that you brought into being. My "baby," *Be Ye Encouraged*, keeps me up at night and it's not even born yet. I spend hours thinking of different ways to announce its imminent arrival. Like all new mothers, I want everyone to come and coo over my perfect little darling.

Publicity and marketing is a major task. Who do I contact first? Will they respond positively? Have I done enough to get the word out? You read everything you can get your hands on about publicity and you ask everyone for ideas. It's trial and error and you learn from your mistakes. The marketing pains are challenging, but expected before this wonderful new life can be born. You take one step at a time.

CHRISTIE GLASCOE CROWDER

After several failed attempts at writing my own press release, I scraped up enough cash to hire a PR agent for two weeks to get the juices flowing. I am a very creative person, when it comes to other people and things, but when I have to talk about myself I go completely blank.

Under the tutelage of my publisher, I created a plan that coincided with the 9-month plan she laid out for all of the MWPC members. Looking at those tasks made me hyperventilate but I used her guidelines to create a schedule for myself, and to my surprise I have beat my own deadlines.

KATHRYN MAHONEY

I'm too cheap (and broke) to hire a PR agent. And the more I talked to different authors, it seemed like the return on investment for hiring an agent wasn't significant enough to warrant it. Many times, it was almost counter-productive. I'm sure each individual scenario is different, but because I have a marketing background I decided to "go it alone" and see what happened.

I didn't do any readings. Something I learned about myself—I'm funny on paper, but when it comes to getting up and speaking in front of people, I'm petrified.

Well, unfortunately, the birth of my book was a little premature. I signed with my publisher in April and started promoting it in September/October. I felt like I was always stuck behind the eight ball trying to learn how to promote the book while promoting it at the same time. If I ever write a second book, I know what to expect and will be more prepared.

CAROLINE POSER

Winter 2006—I feel overwhelmed because of all the major publicity and other events and things that everyone in the co-op is doing. I can't even keep up with reading all the messages on our Yahoo email list.

Fall 2006—I work at home now. I look back to winter and think what a crazy time it was, working full time, commuting an hour-plus each way, daycare in the opposite direction of work, three kids, one only six months-old. No wonder I was exhausted and overwhelmed! But it was observing the baby that reminded me why I needed to publish the book. It's amazing how quickly we forget (maybe that is why many of us have more than one child). Having a baby IS a huge life-changing and important time. *MotherMorphosis* should be honored and celebrated. I owed it to myself to promote my book.

ARLENE SCHUSTEFF

Surprisingly, marketing didn't make me nervous. I'm a big list-making person and I just looked at it like a major checklist that I had to get through. At that point I still didn't have the emotional involvement that it was my "baby." I felt like it was more of a job. I didn't get emotionally attached until I had my book in hand.

Because I had a marketing background, this part was easy for me. Like I said, I just methodically went about it. It never occurred to me—what if someone hates it, what if someone doesn't want to review it, what if someone doesn't want to have a book signing, what if I get a bad review. It didn't occur to me while I had a positive momentum going. It occurred to me after the fact, after I had sent out all the review copies and made all the phone calls, it occurred to me—shit, what if no one likes this. What if I gave them a review copy and they hated it?

PAM LEO

One of the mistakes I made was the money I paid for a professional PR agent. I knew I had to do it right–the mistake was in my timing. I couldn't keep up with the things she needed me to do. I felt I didn't get value for my money because I wasn't ready.

MAUREEN FOCHT

I remember feeling totally overwhelmed. I still feel it's a very complex business. Trying to find PR people to help you can be very, very confusing. I wasted a lot of money. I hired people–some were helpful, some were not.

TERILEE HARRISON

I try to live a fearless life every day but a marketing plan was new for me. It got under my skin. You have to take one little step at a time. While you have a big list on your marketing plan, it's just doing it one bit at a time. People think writing the book is the big deal. That's nothing. It's what comes afterward that counts. People need to be aware of that. Get help, even if you hire a virtual assistant to help send review copies and press releases out for you. Hire a publicist, whether it's a little publicist or big, because it's hard for us to toot our own horn. And you just have to get out there and do it every day.

MALONDA RICHARD

I am so petrified about the next 6 months because I know that my life is going to change dramatically once the book is published. I am sure that there will be many sleepless nights. I am also anxious because I just can't wait to see the first copies of my baby. Like any new parent, I'm sure that I am going to want to show it off to anyone who will let me. I might even take loads and loads of pictures of me and my new book so that I won't forget how we looked upon arrival.

I have dreamed of being a published author since I was 12 years old. My father, the late Eddie Myers Johnson, dreamed of becoming a published author but unfortunately he was not able to have his dream come true–he never found a publisher who believed in his book. Fortunately I was able to one who believed in mine. In less than six months my dream of becoming a published author will come true and my father's dream will be realized through me.

I recently had a strategy meeting with my publicity team and I was surprised at the amount of work that I will have to do during the next six months. Giving birth to a book is just like giving birth to a baby; it requires so much preparation in order to ensure that everyone can be ready. I guess you could say that a publicist is a labor coach.

I have hired Style-Root PR (style-root.com), a small public relations boutique in Brooklyn, NY, to help me develop a major marketing plan for my book. After my first meeting with them I was amazed at all of the possibilities and avenues that we can use to promote and sell the book.

I had no idea that marketing a book would require a talented PR team and a major plan. Initially I was inspired by the plan and then a month later I lost the inspiration to follow through on some of the goals. Thank goodness the plan is on paper and I have a publicist who won't let me fall off of the wagon too many times.

SAMANTHA GIANULIS

In reviewing my original marketing plan, I was a bit reluctant to ask for help. I felt like I should instinctively know how to do a PR campaign—like I should have known what to do when I brought my first child home from the hospital, even though I had never done it before. I hate to say I didn't even know where to start, but it's true.

DEBORAH HURLEY

There were moments along my journey that I felt bitter and angry that I had never received help from connections of any kind. All I had accomplished had been on my own and although I was proud, I also felt angry at times. I was frustrated that I didn't know anyone who worked for a newspaper, or a radio station, or who knew someone who knew someone who could possibly help me promote myself and my book. Everything I had done had been all on my own and I couldn't believe how hard it all was.

NANCY C. CLEARY

I am anxious and apprehensive about the six months ahead. I empathize with all of my authors. This is not an easy endeavor. It's not just the planning of the marketing and publicity, but the realization that if your efforts are successful, you will actually have to "get out there"—your name, your ideas, your face could be everywhere.

I have hired Christine Hohlbaum, one of our member who offers PR consulting, to help me get my marketing plan together. She will help me pitch my ARCs, and, in general, do what she does best—make connections, first in her brilliant mind which networks people together from opposite ends of the earth who share a common theme, and then physically with an introduction, letter, call, or comment that she communicates in the most generous, what's-in-it-for-you way!

Another member, Malonda Richard, is using her creative videography talents to make an *A Book is Born* "book trailer" for my website. Co-Op members were asked to shoot video footage of everything from receiving their books to interview questions. With the upsurge of "book trailers" (just like a movie trailer except for a book) I think all authors should be working this medium into their press kits.

Speaking of press kits, I have signed on with Press Kit 24/7 to host a site for *A Book is Born*. I don't have the budget to hire a pro for a year, so this is the closest I can get—there, my vital information will be at the fingertips of the major media searching for compelling interview guests.

For almost a decade I have watched my authors struggle with book events. Signings at bookstores required a ton of energy to promote, and even with a good turnout, the amount of money made through royalties when you sell through a major retailer is small. It's hardly worth the financial investment unless you look at the "bigger picture" of expanding your visibility more than your profit. Spending a bunch of money and effort to host book launch parties—while they are fun and an ego-boost, puts a dent in the final profit statement. Instead, for our "book tour" we're going to use FreeConferenceCall.com and host a nationwide series of *local* telecalls in an attempt to gather writers and authors together to meet each other and talk about the publishing process. Each host will suggest a meeting place for the call participants—a bookstore, coffee house or living room—and a small community of writers will gather around their copies of *A Book is Born*, following the steps, sharing their experiences, and offering one another support.

The co-op will also launch a blog tour we hope will reach into the online cultures of moms around the world and inspire them to spread the all-powerful "word-of-mom."

More **Tech Tips** from the co-op's Yahoo email list, answered by members who have worked in the PR industry.

Q: To Hire a professional PR agent.. or not?

A: Someone asked me today if she should hire a publicist as she had heard I was rather against hiring someone. I believe the best promoter of the work is the artist himself.

Of course, if you have the resources to hire someone who believes in your project, then go for it. As a PR consultant, I believe in teaching people to fish versus feeding them for a day.

There are MANY publicists out there who do little more than send a few emails and then bill their clients. While there are no guaranteed placements in PR (there are those who sell pay-for-placement but your ROI is very low with such programs), the author herself stands a much better chance of conveying the message with passion than someone for hire. The question to ask is, "Will I achieve my personal and financial goals by hiring this person?"

I admire, honor and respect people in the PR business. It is important, however, to manage your expectations of what a publicist can do for you.

A: I live in the land of the publicists and to be honest there are only a few I like who live in New York, and a few who live outside of the city. Those women do exactly what they should be doing, and they usually exceed their client's expectations. They don't take your money per project, or on a retainer basis, and then only refer you ProfNet notices. They don't take your money and then tell you the press release along with a really expensive press kit is the only way to get yourself into XYZ paper, and they definitely don't ignore your phone calls unless its time for you to pay for the next month.

You see, it's really easy to become a publicist. But it takes *a lot* to become a *good* publicist, and there are very few good ones. I hear more horror stories about people losing money than getting great results. (Of course, the same thing happens in many other industries!)

I know a publicist who works on a per placement basis and he delivers—and then the client delivers him a big fat check at the end of each month. I am not totally against people who choose that way of paying for publicity; they have expectations and the publicist is getting paid for meeting them. I'm just against the pay for placement publicists who cattle call people for the placement and then after you pay, you realize it's for this tiny little misspelled sentence in the *Bumblestick Times* that isn't online and didn't even mention your book. In all honesty, Bumblestick's population of 203 isn't going to help book sales, so why pay for a placement like that?

In some cases, it's best to not have a publicist working for you and other times, you need ANYONE else BESIDES you making the calls. If you get a publicist and she knows your book project like the back of her hand, she will find a thousand ways to pitch you to her already established connections and find great ways to introduce you to other contacts. I don't believe there's anything wrong with a publicist sending a few emails if they are emails to people who don't usually read emails from people they don't know—so she got you in the door, and I'm all for that.

I have so much going on that the idea of having a publicist to take care of one aspect of all my headaches would be lovely... but it's just not worth it for me to take time away from everything to find someone, explain everything, and make sure things are going as planned.

Oh yeah, and the opposite of a publicist who does nothing for you is that really annoying publicist who is extremely pushy and who media hate to get an email or voicemail from. Then you have to worry about undoing the damage they did with contacts you need.

This week *Big Apple Parent* included my book cover when the Editor in Chief reviewed it. Did a publicist do that? Nope. So we all don't *need* one, but if we all found nice ones, I'm sure we would have more time for things we'd rather do during the day!

A: My tip is to lay a foundation first, before you hire a professional. There is so much you can do to be prepared—having a thriving website, a clear author brand and platform, even local media success to show you can perform when you are finally ready to hire a pro for the big bucks to get you national visibility. Remember to think proportionally—you don't want to pay thousands if you won't be selling thousands of books, only national TV sells books in the thousands, and you can only get large, national venues after you've proved yourself on smaller ones.

CHAPTER 4

The Birth

Holding my Baby

*W*HAT IS THE FEELING OF SEEING YOUR your name on the cover of a book? It's an adrenaline rush beyond compare. Every time you spy your baby you stare proudly at what you have created. All of it came out of you; it's you for the world to see.

I asked the co-op members how they felt when they received their books, and who they gave the first copies to. And, just like any new mom, there are tons of questions for the newbie author—a few are answered in Tech Tips.

"I couldn't stop grinning for about a month after the delivery! I felt like I had achieved such an accomplishment. I was a proud momma of a bouncing baby book! It felt like a dream come true."

IN THIS CHAPTER

Beholding our books for the first time

Tech Tips – Questions from newbie authors

Funny Publishing Stats

Beholding our books for the first time

KATHRYN MAHONEY

I couldn't stop grinning for about a month after the delivery! It was such an accomplishment, a dream come true. I was a proud momma of a bouncing baby book. I don't think many writers are 100% confident that other people actually want to read their work, but by getting the support and blessing of my publisher, I felt like perhaps this is the path God wanted me to follow. Perhaps people really were interested in what I had to say.

The birth of a book is definitely like the birth of a baby. As soon as it enters the world you forget about the nine months of previous aches, pains, and weight gain that got you to this point. You just want to hold the book and smile, and that's what I did for months.

The first copies went to my husband and children and they were just as happy as I was. The next copies went to my sister because she helped proofread and edit the book, and then of course to my mother and father because after all, they gave birth to the author. Everybody was very proud of me and I'm not going to deny that it felt good!

PAULA SCHMITT

The day my books were delivered to my front door was a day I will never forget. I couldn't wait to tear open the box and hold one in my hands. After FedEx arrived with the delivery I carried the heavy box up to my room, cut open the packaging, held one of MY books in my hands and tears came to my eyes—I was overwhelmed with happiness. I was so proud that I had accomplished what I had set out to do—to write a book and have it published.

The first copy of my book went to my boys. They are so proud of the cover—they ARE the cover of the book, and they remind me quite frequently that is the reason the book will sell.

CHRISTINE LOUISE HOHLBAUM

Who did I give the first copy to? It was the post lady. No kidding. It was a sunny June morning. The birds were chirping, the children were hopping about the yard, and the post lady greeted me at my picket fence.

"Sign here," she said, rather unceremoniously. I looked at the package then threw my arms around her neck!

NINA MARIE DURAN

I got my books and I don't think I'm EVER gonna get off this HIGH! They are beautiful...actually, beautiful doesn't even touch them! They're beautiful beyond words.

The first person I gave it to was my mom, and she cried. She was so happy. She said, "You did it!"

Opening my box of books was the best labor without an epidural. My first thought when I saw them—"Oh my God. I did it!" It was a sense of self-accomplishment which, to me, was one of the best feelings ever. When I saw my book I felt worthy.

ARLENE SCHUSTEFF

Upon receiving my books I felt a combination of so many different emotions. I was anxious, I was excited, I was nervous. I was an emotional wreck waiting for them. I thought they would be arriving on a certain day, but a week earlier I came home and there was a pile of boxes! My heart started beating fast. It was now tangible. The most exciting part for me was when I opened the boxes my kids were there, and they were so excited. They want to take books across the street to to show them off. The funny thing is—the book is really about them, but they have no intention to read it, they just wanted it.

PAMELA JO LEO

When my book arrived I just held it and cried. I remember when my oldest child Brandy, was born, she was covered with my tears as I held her the first time. I couldn't believe that something that incredible could have come out of me. I felt the same way when I held my book in my hands. I muttered softly, "I did it, I really, really did it. This is my baby!"

I gave my first copy to my mom. She hugged me, and then she wanted to buy it! I said "No, no Mom." But she made me take the money so she could be the first person to buy my book.

MAUREEN FOCHT

Receiving my books was fantastic. To be honest I thought it would be thicker. I started thinking, "I guess I should have written more." As I looked through it though—it was perfect!

Most people were surprised and impressed. A few gasped, "Oh my gosh, you wrote a book?" and it was like they put me on a pedestal. Most people are thrilled to get a personally signed copy by the author. It's great for your ego!

TERILEE HARRISON

My Dad lives in Ohio, and I see him once every two years. But by chance, he was in California visiting me for 48 hours and was here the day the big truck arrived! We had the camera on as my family was pushing the palette up the driveway (because, of course, I didn't just order one case of books.) My husband opened a box and pulled a book out—it was such an incredible experience. *And* I had 100 moms who contributed to the book to share this feeling—they were all anxiously awaiting their copies!

I started to hand my dad a copy and he said he already ordered it on Amazon. That was so cute. My daughter said, "Well, I'm taking mine." And she took it to her room, and for a couple weeks after that she snuck it out of the house to show her friends. Even today, six months later, it still sits by her bed, on her nightstand. At an age when your child thinks you are weird, to have her be so proud of something I did, means so much to me.

MARNA KRAJESKI

How did it feel when I first saw my baby? Surreal. I would compare it to the feeling when you find out are pregnant for the first time. It's a delicious, heady experience, sort of wonderment.

CAROLINE POSER

My boxes were at the side door! I hauled them in this morning, but the sad thing was I couldn't open them until six hours later. I knew if I did I would lose my focus on work and tomorrow is the last day of the quarter so I am under big pressure. I came home this evening after having picked up the three kids, hauling in them and all their stuff. The big boys saw the boxes and squealed, "What are those, Mommy?" (thinking *they* got something). I told them, "It's Mommy's book, want to see?" They muttered, "No...." and went in to watch TV, waiting for me to serve them dinner. So I opened up a box and took a book out and showed it to the baby.

I am very excited, yet at the same time, utterly exhausted. The ironic thing is, I haven't felt this way since I had the baby last summer! I didn't even think about it until I got to this paragraph, that that sentiment fits right in with the theme of *A Book is Born*.

I know now my promo work has barely begun. I need to make it through tomorrow, and then I will have all weekend to regroup and refocus on my *new* baby, if the real baby and big boys cooperate.

JULIE WATSON SMITH

I'd like to say my first feeling was pride, but it was shock, followed by confidence. It's a great feeling to know that someone outside your inner realm has faith in you. It also shocks you into realizing that you need to perform!

The very first copy I gave out was to my babysitter who responded with tears and hugs. She was one of the individuals I acknowledged in my book. Her tireless enthusiasm and love for my children gave me the comfortable space to work on *Mommyhood Diaries*.

ALANA MORALES

I hate to say this, but I felt disappointment. There was a miscommunication about the book—I did not know what I was asked to approve was going to press already—and the foreword and dedication were not in there. The book was dedicated to my late grandfather, who was a symbol of hard work and determination, and I was crushed. It was by far the biggest disappointment in my life. When something is that anticipated and you get it and it's not like you expect, it's a very hard thing to stomach.

DEBORAH HURLEY

It's December 13th at 8:15 pm and I gave birth! Okay, who heard me screaming? I had one of the busiest days of my life. Both kids had religion class, one at 4:00 and the other at 7:00, my daughter had a horseback riding lesson at 5:00 and my son had a hockey game at 6:30. My husband is at a Christmas dinner tonight so I had to find a way to divide myself in three and figure out how to get everyone where they needed to go. We finally pulled into the driveway at 8:30 pm and, to our surprise, the front porch was stacked with beautiful brown boxes. My daughter flew into the house and grabbed the video camera and for a minute I realized how the three of us were sharing a special moment in time. What I had once thought would never happen has and it's incredible! They are perfect!

I'm going to put my PJs on now and go stare at my books.

IRIS WAICHLER

I remember feeling like a stalker as I watched and waited for the delivery truck carrying my book to arrive. I am sure the FedEx man was surprised, and perhaps a little frightened, when I burst out of my front door and flew toward him to help him unload the truck.

LEEDA BACON

My book is here! Oh my gosh, it's here! My "baby" is finally here after all the preparation, pomp and circumstance. A labor of love—also plain labor.

I felt the excitement of birth pangs when I heard the roar of the big brown truck racing down the street then rolling up in front of my house. My heart pounded; it was delivery time.

When I opened the door, the UPS driver exclaimed with great exuberance, "Your book is here!" Eager to help make the dream of seeing my baby a reality, she quickly handed me the necessary form for my signature then ran back to the truck for the precious cargo. Just as a skilled, compassionate nurse or midwife shares in the excitement of bringing a little one into the world, this delivery woman did as well. She meticulously gathered each box and carefully wheeled them to the threshold. As I stood watching, I thought about the days, even months, of sleepless nights when this unborn baby would wake me from a sound sleep with ideas that would pop into my head and I would have to get up and write them down.

The smiling driver placed one of the boxes in my hands and said, "Congratulations!" She then piled the others inside and waited to see the bundle of joy as I scissored open the cardboard. Gazing upon my baby she cooed, "Oh, it's beautiful! I'm so excited for you! Good luck!" I felt like a new mom, caressing what had become the focus of my life the last nine months, and would change my world forever. Now the real work begins.

MALONDA RICHARD

My books arrived today so it is official...YEAH! I am now officially a published author! Wow. Now I have to sell them.

SAMANTHA GIANLUIS

I had read, re-read, edited, re-wrote, and mercilessly reviewed my own book prior to release. I loved my book one day, hated it the next. I remembered a movie scene about loathing our own work that described my state of mind sometimes.

"Teaching is a way of paying the rent until I finish my novel."

"How long have you been writing it?"

"Ten years."

"It must be very good."

"It's a piece of shit."

(Tom Hulce and Donald Sutherland in *Animal House*)

People would ask, "How's the book coming along?" I was tempted to say, "It's a piece of shit," but I remembered that honest people, well-read people, and the writers I knew, liked it. They told me it was good. So I went with it.

One hour ago, a guy wearing all brown dropped off two cardboard boxes...my baby, my book, my goal, sat there staring at me. Once again, Zoë sang her made up song "Little Grapes on the Vine/Little Grapes on the Vine/Mama wrote about Little Grapes on the Vine."

I didn't smell shit, I smelled success. It is sweet. But it's still not real to me; I disbelieve what I am seeing, two inches away from my hand. If she (the book) were a real baby, I'd say I hope she is happy, always happy, and healthy. I hope she brings happiness to others, brings them health through my recipes, and makes food into wonderful memories for them.

I love my baby more than I thought I could because I am hyper-critical of myself. I know I will be judged, I will be scrutinized for what I have written, it's inevitable. But right now, I just don't care! Right now, I'm feeling pretty good. I did something I set out to do, bestseller or not. Furthermore, I believe in what I did. I love those words and the recipes.

If this book were not meant to be, I wouldn't be writing this and you wouldn't be reading it.

The cloud I am on resembles a cluster of grapes. I don't see it but I believe there is an invisible vine leading me to special things ahead. And I will have everyone else in MWPC to thank, in addition to those who love me, because they all let me shine, even when I said the sun wasn't out. How could it not have been out? Grapes need sunlight to grow.

JENNIFER KALITA

Receiving my books felt like a dream realized. I knew one day I would write a book, but to do so this early in my life, and to have written something so well received, is at once elating and humbling. And now I have the fever...I can't wait to start the next book!

Questions from newbie authors

Book Events

Q: I have my first book signing tonight! Based on friends, and what the owner tells me, I expect about 30 people. About how long should I speak/read? I prepared a little opening thing and then I was planning to read 2 or 3 essays. Is that enough or should I do more? What has worked for you in the past? I don't want to be too long, but want to give them something substantial. Thanks.

A: I'd say read two of your punchiest essays. Be sure to talk informally a bit before you read. Set up the stories and give the audience a sense for your voice. Then transition between stories and say a little bit after the second one. This gives the audience a breather to process and formulate any questions they may have (no awkward silences.) Have a glass of water handy. Audiences are always interested in the writing/publishing process too. Hope this helps!

Q: Would some of you be willing to share how your book launch party was? I'm thinking about having one and want to begin planning it now. How long was yours? Did you have any giveaways? How many people came? Any creative ideas? Any info or input would be great! Thanks everyone.

A: My book launch was a blast. I focused it on being a "mom's night out." We had food, drinks, raffles, and favor bags. I tied the book launches into a cause, St. Vincent de Paul's Village, benefiting homeless families. Then I donated a portion of all sales to St. Vincent's as well. I also asked that each person attending bring a canned good or non-perishable item to restock the food banks. I ended up with mounds and mounds of diapers, canned goods, and more. It was great! My most successful event was the first which we did at a Mexican restaurant with food and drinks. Rest your voice because you'll be doing a lot of talking!

A: I had one in LA two weeks ago and have another scheduled in Orange County this coming Tuesday. In LA it was at a friend's restaurant. We had appetizers and wine. I had about 60 people. They all sat and visited and worked the room. Everyone loved it. It started at 6:30 pm and it seemed to have an early wave of people, and then a later wave. We left at 9:30 pm.

The OC one this Tuesday is at Little Black Dress Jewelry's show-room. It will be more of an open house from 4 to 8 pm. And I am sure after they get their book signed, they will be visiting and looking at the jewelry. (www.lbdjewelry.com) I am expecting 40 or so.

At the parties, I offered a discount price if they bought 3 books or more. Several people took advantage of it.

A: I had my book launch party in conjunction with a send-off for my husband, who was leaving for Afghanistan the following month. We had it at the Alumni Center at the University of RI, where Paul worked in the ROTC department. About 100 people (including Senator Jack Reed!) showed up. I signed books in the conference room. Midway through the evening, Paul gave a little speech and I read a story about him from my book.

Since the Send-Off was the day before Armed Forces Day, we also had a fundraiser for Fisher House in conjunction with the event. Fisher Houses are like Ronald McDonald houses, but they are located near major military medical centers. They provide low-cost lodging for military families who are looking after a sick or injured service member (www.fisherhouse.org). Our guests, at the end, donated money (some were very generous) and I gave $2 for each book sold that night. Altogether, we raised $1000!

I wrote a press release about the donation, which netted some additional publicity for the Fisher House foundation and *Household Baggage*. The VP at Fisher House provided me with a nice quotation for the release. A lot of folks, including our Army friends, had never heard of the Fisher Houses, so I was glad we helped get the word out. It is a wonderful organization.

A: I recommend building relationships with local radio producers to help promote your events and book launches. Their contact information is very easy to obtain via the internet—and you could become a repeat guest easily. It's been my strategy and has worked well. Try going to www.radio-locator.com (more about how to pitch to radio stations in *The Author's Companion*, see resource section for more info) to find stations near you and your target audience to build the buzz abut your upcoming book events.

Hate Mail & Bad Reviews

Q: Just curious, has anyone ever gotten hate mail? I had two emails from different people and both were quite nasty. The first guy said that I was trying to promote "substandard" parenting and that I was setting a bad example for young mothers. Ouch. The second was about my second book, and said that I was, "...exploiting the pain of those struggling," and she hoped that, "there was a special place in hell for me." I know this comes with the turf, but I gotta admit, it freaked me out and I can't stop thinking about it. Anyone ever dealt with this before?

A: Wow, that stinks about the hate mail, but you could look at it that you are popular enough to create controversy!

A: I did get a letter from a woman about an article I wrote where she felt I didn't understand her infertility pain. I wrote her back and addressed some of her comments and explained where I was coming from. She ended up writing me back several times and became quite a fan. I think she appreciated me taking the time to address her fears. I am not suggesting you get in touch with the one that told you go to hell, but you might consider addressing the first email. You may end up with a convert. Good luck.

A: My friend Chelle Campbell, the author of *The Wealthy Spirit*, says to move forward and to become famous, we have to be willing to be both totally LOVED and occasionally HATED. (Just concentrate on the love!)

A: Everyone will have their own opinions about what you do. Sometimes the best response is, "I strive for perfection but I keep coming up human every time."

A: One of my biggest fears is getting negative feedback about my book. At this time I can only speak from life experience about people's negative comments and hurtful words. It's so easy to get caught up in the negativity people spew at us because naturally we would like to please everyone. What I've learned how to do is think about all that I have accomplished, all the good that I have done, and all the positive feedback that I have gotten. Focus only on those you have enlightened and helped and dismiss everything else. I use negativity as fuel that pushes me forward, turning it into a positive. I realize that when someone says something hurtful, the person behind those words is most likely bitter and angry. I feel sorry for people who have to be cruel to others but I don't waste any time on them.

A: I really appreciated the other comments. I have one more thought about hate mail issue. I can't help it, it's the social worker in me. People are angry and sound bitter for many reasons. Sometimes the topics we are writing about such as parenting, or infertility in my case, hit vulnerable and painful areas for people. People's experiences in these areas may not be positive. The anger they vent towards us has nothing to do with what we write but perhaps our writing reconnects them with events or memories they would rather not be reminded of. The woman who initially wrote me a negative letter ultimately wrote me back to apologize and tell me though she sounded "crazy" when she first wrote me she was not. She later explained the pain of ongoing infertility would overwhelm her sometimes and admitted she took it out on me. We ended on a really positive note and she thanked me for what I wrote and for taking the time to respond and listen to what she had to say. I was glad I did. This is just a long-winded way of saying not to personalize the comments or let them deter you from working on a project you really believe in.

A: What wonderful advice and support everyone has given. I not only agree wholeheartedly but think we should not let other people's hang-ups discourage us from what we were meant to do. And if your work did not have an audience, a purpose, and a benevolent message then it would not be out there. I haven't gone through this yet but I am attempting to grow some thicker skin, as publishing personal things is a bit like putting our souls on the chopping block. Hang in there! Composure is sexy.

Distribution

Q: Forgive me for still not understanding how this works, but I do not understand how our book distributor works. I went into Borders yesterday, spoke with the manager there and she told me that I would need to go online to "New Vendor Acquisitions" and fill out a submissions form. I understand that our distributor presents our books to bookstores, but does each individual bookstore decide whether they want to carry them or not? Which bookstores does our distributor present our books to? Could you please explain this to me?

A: Thanks for asking, I'll answer (this is Nancy)—let's break this down piece by piece.

First, my suggestion when approaching bookstore staff, maybe with your bookmark in hand, is to tell them, "Hi, I'm a local author, my book comes out in January and I will be doing a bunch of local media so I wanted to let you know, in case you'd like to have some on hand." And hand them the bookmark which has your distributor's name listed.

It sounds like the manager is under the impression that you do not have a distributor. Here's a side lesson—I can't tell you how many store clerks have given authors a hard time, and it makes me wonder, do wanna-be authors work at bookstores? And if so, do they hold a grudge for all new authors?

Second, whenever you speak with a manager or sales clerk at a bookstore you can simply give them your title and/or ISBN and they will call it up on their computer. Bookstores have different programs; one is "iPage"—and when they punch in the ISBN they will see who distributes your book. Our distributor just officially became the biggest, so for them to give you directions as they did sounds like they assumed you self-published without a major bookstore distributor.

Third, your book won't ship until mid-December, so if they are under the impression it should be available now you should say it comes out in January (this is listed on the computer as well.)

Fourth, the distributor submits your sell sheets, excerpts, cover, and publicity reports to their regional reps who in turn either order for their regional sellers (who represent the individual store buyers) or supply directly to the chains. Borders buys directly from our distributor, as does Barnes & Noble and Amazon. Others buy from Ingram or Baker & Taylor, who order from our distributor.

If you do not have big local media or national media you may not be on their "radar." And yes, each store can decide if they want to carry a book if they don't automatically get it from the buyers. If you're not a big author chances are the big buyers have not ordered a large "push" for the bookstores. To be in bookstores nationwide requires tens of thousands of books to be "ordered" by the distributor and pushed to major cities (all returnable). Even then, there is still a chance a customer could walk into a bookstore and not see your book on the shelf, but it could be in the store across town!

PLEASE also realize—once the bookstore has your book on the shelf, they will only keep it there for 90 days. Unless you are getting major media, or have become an underground bestseller, they will return it. So, if they are not ordering your books right away, waiting until you do have big media would be advantageous to you.

I know it can be challenging—but we work incredibly hard to be with a major distributor, and believe me, we are tiny in comparison, that's why I keep saying we are "playing with the big-hitters."

Here's what you do—we get you some national media and you go dancing back into that snobby store like Julia Roberts, and go up to the manager and say, "I'll be on Dr. Phil next week, so you might want to get some of my books in stock...or it'll be a big, huge mistake," and then go dancing out.

Celebrity Endorsements

Q: Got a question for everyone who has ever sought a celebrity endorsement. I am going after a couple of different people, have googled their publicists, and come up with nothing. Has anybody ever used those "Contact Celebrities" websites, in which you pay to get that coveted info.

A: Yes, I've used contactanycelebrity.com, and it was worth the money. This is the most effective and efficient way to get a celebrity's agent/manager/publicist info. When writing, try to frame your requests around a cause. For example, Sarah Jessica Parker favors homeless causes. If you don't have a cause, think of an angle that can be used for good publicity for the celebrity—maybe Rachel Ray wants to reach out more to parents, or perhaps, Molto Mario has a soft spot for moms.

Bookstore Signings

Q: Anybody want to share their ideas/experiences on getting book signings? I have a friend with a friend who manages one of the big Borders in my town, and I was wondering...should I call? Stop in with my press release, sell sheet, maybe an ARC?

A: Stop by with your darling smile and thrust an ARC under his nose. When you are face to face, it is harder to say no. He may wish to order a copy himself, but I'd say go for it. Leverage your contacts and let him know it's a win-win.

A: In my experience, you will do a LOT better financially by finding your own spot and publicizing your signing—you will make next to nothing selling your books at Borders. They are making the profit, and you are making a very small royalty. That's not to say you don't want them to have your book, of course. Your first signing is the best! Send an invite to absolutely everyone you know, and have some goodies, maybe wine, etc. It's your day—don't give it all to Borders. And your local paper will love to feature you as a local published author.

A: If it's a big-city Borders they're probably scheduled full with larger authors. I might suggest you bring a review pack to your friend's friend in person—with ARC, sell sheet, and a pitch letter that highlights your media and sells what your event would be about. Tell him when you are scheduling events, and ask if he could pass the information on to the "Community Relations Manager" or "Events Manager"—tell him you'd love to schedule an event, or at least be a back-up if they need one.

A: In my limited experience, I found that even Barnes and Noble sometimes would do a little more for local authors. Also, if you do an author event somewhere else so you can demonstrate you are appearing around town, or have a good review in hand with your materials and information, that can be helpful as well.

Follow Up

Q: How many times do you follow up with someone before you give up? I sent ARCs to a few places that I think are perfect that have done book reviews or run excerpts before. I called once and emailed three times. Still no response. At what point am I becoming a stalker?

A: The key is to plant as many seeds as you possibly can. I made the mistake of hounding reviewers after my first book came out—the result? Virtually zero reviews from my oh-so promising leads. Consider your book promotion journey like a garden—you cultivate, nurture and weed out what doesn't work. It takes lots of time, contacts, patience and a huge dose of humor. A friendly, "I just wanted to share what the Podunk Review said about my latest book in the event Uncle Earl didn't tell you," may give people something to laugh about. It is nerve-wracking to wait so my advice is—don't. Keep moving forward, passing out postcards, business cards and bookmarks. It will make the difference if you do!

Radio

Q: I know about "Radio Locator" to find out contact info at stations. However, how do I narrow down which to target? How do I know which stations have shows that might be compatible with my book? Has anyone had any success with a certain station? I am kind of at a loss on how to contact stations, and I don't want to contact those who wouldn't be interested in a book like mine. Any advice?

A: Radio locator gives you loads of options. Your best bet is to go for those stations with a broader reach (measured in WATTS.) Look at each individual website before pitching. Knowing the format can make the difference between a "no" and a "yes."

A: We've talked about paying a fee for radio interviews. A colleague sent me an email offering his services. While his list of clients is impressive, his fees are equally astounding. I'm not saying he is not valid. I think he is. But this gives you a taste of what people are charging.

Here's what he wrote in response to my query about what he meant by "low" fee: Fees range from $600-$1975 per interview based upon air time for shows running coast to coast on over 60 radio stations plus the Internet. (As an aside, I have been on NPR eleven times with over 165 radio stations airing the show and it cost me nothing.)

This brings up a great subject of cost versus benefit. My opinion is to pay as little as you can while still getting the exposure you deserve. In my experience, a tiny AM station in Montana may not offer you the exposure you're looking for (unless you are a fly-fisher!) If you get the interview, you may wish to consider it just to practice your message. If you have to pay for it, however, it may not be worth your time or money.

Often the fees are more than the actual royalties you receive. Pay for placement needs to be carefully considered. Would you pay to be on *Oprah*? Maybe, because the ROI (return on investment) is generally very high. Would you pay to be on NPR? I would not. Why? Because you can get on with little to no investment if you know how to work with the media.

Then again, you may view your media experience in terms of "platform building" and then the media fee is worthwhile. You can then claim you are a sought-after speaker with X number of media interviews. You thereby build your   status as an expert and people begin to refer to you as one. It depends on what it is worth to you. PR is never guaranteed, no matter what some people might promise you. At the same time, you can build your own empire with very few resources without having to pay someone else an exorbitant fee.

TV

Q: I'm getting ready to send out another round of review copies to radio and TV people. There are so many...does anyone know if any of them are easier to get to? I'm not really sure how to narrow down the list outside of the Chicago area. Also, if I want to send to places like *The View* or the *Today Show*, who do I send it to? A producer? I know I have to pitch it as part of a bigger story, but I'm not sure who to send to at the places that are not on the contact list. Don't want to do a lot of random sending. Any advice in this area would be appreciated and if anyone has a hot contact, please let me know!

A: National TV producers like to see "clips" or videotaped segments of you on smaller shows to determine what type of guest you will be. Try getting a few producers interested in the Chicago area first with a local pitch. Get a sample clip from those shows and send them to larger producers with a national pitch, including the Chicago-based *Oprah* show!

Q: The number one person on my list who I am seeking an endorsement from is Dr. Phil. I know he may be way out of my league but I'm still going to try. His interests are in helping to make families stronger, healthier and more connected to each other, and my book offers hope to women suffering from depression, and helps bring them back to their children, husbands and families. Without a healthy mom, children suffer.

So does anyone know of a way to convince Dr. Phil to look at me and my work, other than just mailing my ARC? Is there any way I can get in touch with a producer of the show to ask how difficult it is to get an appointment with him? Or do I just mail my ARC to his studio and hope for the best? There is no info on producers or anyone in his studio on his website.

A: The best way to work yourself into the good graces of Dr. Phil, Oprah, or any of the talk show or news producers is to respond to their online queries, as well as participate in their discussion boards (in an educational, non-self-promotional way) when their show topic matches your platform.

They really don't care about you individually (sorry), only about putting together great programs, where you could potentially be a perfect guest. You have to spin your story, your pitch, and your ideas to match their query for a show in the works, and be prepared to act in whatever capacity they need. You must be succinct yet emotional in your responses. If your passion and wisdom come through, you could very likely receive an email or call asking you for more info, a video, or a phone interview. I have personally received three responses to online queries I have submitted to Oprah.com (a fraction of the hundred sent over the last 8 years!)

One member received a book request from a combination of responding to a query and posting a press release about the topic tied to a current tragedy in the news. Another member received a call from a query she completed. That's some pretty darn good odds considering how many tens of thousands of emails the shows receive daily. Only a fraction of the queries get responses, assistants to the assistants probably spend less than 3 seconds scanning each one. While none have ever worked out for us, we are certainly on their radar! The bigger you build your platform, the more times the producers see your name in more places, the more likely the chance they will recognize it when you submit to one of their online queries.

Bookmark these "Be on the Show" pages:
www2.oprah.com/tows/intheworks/tows_works_main.jhtml
www.drphil.com/?letmein=1

A: I didn't have a clue about how to do this until I started talking and learning from people who do know. As Nancy said, I have learned that the pitch is important to catch the attention of the person you are contacting. It needs to have a headline, something that grabs their attention and shows them why you have something unique and special to say about your experience or topic. Then you need some kind of a short list of talking points (about five) . If you think about interviews you've seen on TV or heard on the radio, they often have a short list of tips the author shares with the audience. These tips should be brief but informative. On your pitch sheet have a brief bio about yourself, any experience you have had with the media, and how to contact you by phone and email.

Publishing Stats

Did you know 90% of authors, with or without children, equate publishing their book to having a baby.

Funny stats from the MWPC...

- *4 out of 5 surveyed plead temporary insanity when asked why they wrote their book, or why they had children*

- *70% experience morning sickness at some point; for authors it is during the review process*

- *New authors check their Amazon rankings more than a new mother checks her baby*

- *50% will suffer postpartum depression 90 days after the birth caused from an uneven balance of hormones or book store returns*

- *Authors gain an average of 5.6 pounds a month writing their book and lose 10.2 pounds a month promoting it*

- *30% of authors suffer shock when they realize they receive the equivalent of their child's milk money for each book sold*

- *10% of mom authors publish for the money, the rest do it for bragging rights to their kids*

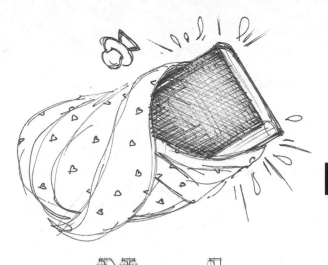

CHAPTER 5

Newborns

Baby for Sale

*S*O, THE BUNDLE OF JOY HAS FOUND A VOICE, and waling through the night is just part of the publicity process. The co-op members share the exhilaration and exhaustion of the first month. Empowerment is coupled with loss of control—your baby has to fend for itself in the Amazon jungle, and when the stores send your books back by the carton you can't help but ask, "What's wrong with my baby?"

Tech Talk encourages wrapping a pitch around anything that happens in your niche, the *biggest* media "get" of all happened when we did.

"My first month has been utterly exciting. I had an author event at the wonderful bookstore where I first got the idea to write the book. I felt like I had come full circle."

IN THIS CHAPTER

The first few months

Tech Talk
Pitch Your Niche

Navigating the Amazon Jungle

Tech Talk
Making the most of Amazon

Returns—is something wrong with my baby?

The first few months

JULIE WATSON SMITH

It was very exhilarating and exhausting. During the first 30 days I had a book launch, four book signings, a television appearance, two print and blog interviews, and a radio segment. Not knowing what the best vehicle was to get the word out about *Mommyhood Diaries*, I tried them all! I found that the best venues for sales were print, internet, radio and the book launch party. Television and book signings didn't generate the same amount of sales, but the appearances provided a platform for additional events.

Joely Fisher, seen here reading her copy of *Mommyhood Diaries* with author Julie Watson Smith and Joely's sister Tricia Fisher, founder of Nana's Garden where the event was held.

Heather Mills and her daughter Beatrice Lilly McCartney can be seen playing at the back table during the event (they were not in attendance, but they were there nonetheless!)

IRIS WAICHLER

My first month has been utterly exciting. I had an author event at the wonderful bookstore where I first got the idea to write the book. I felt like I had come full circle. My friends took me out for dinner and celebrated my success before the author event. Then several more friends and my husband attended the event itself.

Iris Waichler hosts a book signing at Transitions Bookstore in Chicago.

I looked at everyone from the podium and saw smiles and tears in their eyes, and that meant the world to me because I knew my words had touched them deeply. My family and friends have been incredibly supportive and positive about my book. People have called me to say they saw displays of my book in local bookstores and it feels great that they are genuinely happy for me. People who have undergone infertility treatment have told me how deeply the book touched them, which was incredibly gratifying as that was what I had hoped for as I began my book project.

My friends and family have gone to my website and checked out my book on Amazon.com and BarnesandNoble.com. As my publicity has increased, I am getting more comments from people in the community and at my daughter's school. They have been very positive, and some have even shared their infertility stories with me.

I wrote a major article for a local publication here that has a large readership. It went into detail about my infertility background and had large color photos of my family and I. Then I began hearing responses from more people and it really felt like the wider world was now responding to my personal story. I also have begun to get letters from people who have struggled with infertility and bought my book and found it very helpful. Connecting with strangers who have struggled, as I did, and being able to help them is profoundly gratifying for me.

PAULA SCHMITT

Living in a Locker Room launched on May 1, 2005. Sales from my website were high and I was signing and shipping books out to family and friends like crazy. Even people who heard me talking about my book on a local radio show out of Colchester, VT bought copies. I was beaming!

The rest of the month sales were great and I was on cloud nine. I am checking Amazon.com every day for comments and reviews on the book. Lookin' good!

In May I made an appearance on World Talk Radio with Cynthia Brian from Be the Star You Are! I also continued working with my PR agent on publicity by sending more books out to newspapers, magazines and radio shows.

Author of *Living in a Locker Room*, Paula Schmitt's name appears on a marquee to the residents and vacationers in Lake Winnipesauke, New Hampshire.

ALANA MORALES

The first month was good. I had my book launch party, plus several media successes-I was on three of my local news stations and in two local papers in the first few months—and that was fun! I love being in front of the camera and don't really get too nervous. In fact, people still compliment me on my appearances because I seem calm and am having fun.

People think it's cool to meet an author. I actually don't play the author part up as much as I should!

I didn't lose too much sleep with my "newborn." I would get nervous right before the event, but that's it. Losing sleep won't help, but being prepared will. So, I make sure I know what I want to say, then I know that my personality will carry me once I get there.

I received a few fan emails and they made my month! I love knowing that there are people out there who like what I say, and I love feeling like I helped them.

CHRISTINE LOUISE HOHLBAUM

Book signings weren't very practical for me, though I did hold one signing in my hometown the first year I was here in Germany. Even though it was in English, I sold 17 copies to a group of 16 people. Not bad for a room full of German speakers!

Author of *SAHM I Am: Tales of a Stay-at-Home Mom in Europe*, Christine Hohlbaum, seen here with her two children at home in Germany.

Over the past four years, I have been in a lot of major media: NPR (a dozen times), *Woman's Day, Parenting, Parents, Boston Globe* magazine, *Christian Science Monitor,* and more. The first few weeks of a book promotion tour are crucial. Since I had already positioned myself as a mom expert with my first book, launching the second was much easier because everything was already in place. I had a cool website, which my publisher most graciously branded with nifty graphics; I had a strong Internet presence through dozens of parenting articles; and I had start-ed a parenting humor newsletter to hundreds of subscribers. It took a lot of persistence to connect with the right people.

Nothing beats the look of awe people have in their eyes when you tell them you are an author. "Really?" they squeak at cocktail parties and hair salons. It's neat. There are a lot of misconceptions about authors. We may be all crazy, but we aren't all rich.

At one point, a grand disillusionment set in. I thought it would be fairly breezy to get on TV or in the *New York Times*. Ha! What's a writer to do other than write about the experience? I wrote a blog entry, My Imaginary Interview with Oprah, about gaining perspective on the whole book promotion process.

I learned a long time ago to let the words live in the hearts and minds of my readers. The work no longer belongs only to me. Everyone who comes into contact with my writing owns a piece of it too. It used to feel like running naked through an executive board meeting. Now I take people's opinions in stride.

NINA MARIE DURAN

I don't even remember the first month. The only thing I remember was I lost ten pounds and I was so excited. It was tough—I did everything on my own. With HEB (a grocery store chain) I started at the bottom and went through a lot of "you've got to contact this person" and they'd say "no, you've got to contact this person." Finally I got the right person. What's so awesome about San Antonio businesses is they are always eager to help local authors.

I had a lot of connections in TV before hand. I always believed it's not what you know, it's who. There I was, years later, calling all these people and they were all so nice.

KATHRYN MAHONEY

The first month was great. It was like a game to see who would actually publish an article or write a story about the "mother author." And in

many cases, I found that you really just need to ask for publicity. I sent press releases out primarily to local media and to places where I had some history (birthplace, college, etc.) All these publications ran a story about the book and one of the local papers ran nearly a full-page article about the book with a picture of me about the size of my head! Imagine picking up the newspaper at the convenience store and having your face staring back at you. It was freaky, but felt pretty good too!

Author of *Cracked at Birth* Kathryn Mahoney here with her family at book launch in Boston.

PAMELA JO LEO

I'm so bad at promoting myself. So many things that have been in the media were due to other people taking action on my behalf. For example the librarian here in Gorham, Maine set up my first book signing *and* an interview with the local paper that got a full-page spread.

I had this great marketing plan I thought I was going to follow; get up every day and send out emails to parenting web sites and groups, but so much happened in my personal life at that time that I just couldn't do it. There was always this nagging voice in my head "you have to get the book out there" but I had to just do what I could. I felt, "Baby, you are going to have to make it on your own." And it did, my book went on without me. The message is premature for our culture. It's an idea whose time has not yet come, so in that respect I knew I had time, and that people would respond even without me.

DEBORAH HURLEY

I must tell you how Saturday night went. I never thought that so many people cared about me. If I ever had doubts about my book and about all that I have revealed, they are gone. The night began at 6 pm and by 7:30 there were wall-to-wall people. I had a guestbook, which everyone signed, and there were close to 200 people there. There was live music, lots of wine, a positive indescribable energy and yummy treats. I signed endless books, talked with everyone, and was completely blown away by the show of support. The best part was seeing people walk in whom I had never met. They shared stories about loved ones who were sick with depression and they felt compelled to come and meet me. I was touched by every single minute and at one point I just looked around the room and truly felt a much larger presence near me. By 11:00 pm the director of the Art Gallery came to me and told me that she has had many authors do their launches there but she has never seen a crowd like this. She was blown away as well. The Smithtown Chamber of Commerce was there and the man who helps organize the chamber asked me how on earth I did it. He couldn't believe the crowd either.

Dr. Wolpert from London emailed me to wish me luck. I feel certain that what we have put together will help so many who are suffering. There are no magic answers in my book, but I do believe it will provide someone with a ray of light.

Author of *Fragments of Hope*, Debbie Hurley signs books at her NY launch party.

I have waited my entire life to give the way that I am giving now. I will not take one moment of it for granted.

MARNA KRAJESKI

I was fortunate that my book launch got wrapped into a news story about my husband's departure to Afghanistan. A reporter from the *Providence Journal* interviewed us both, so there was a nice story and a IIUGE color picture of us in the local section. Below it was a sidebar story about my book with the cover. It was great publicity. I had also given the reporter a news release with "Ten Ways You Can Support Someone When Her Spouse is Deployed." This release, along with a picture of the book, was in the Sunday edition. Statewide coverage—what a thrill!

JENNIFER KALITA

Surprising. I was ranked in Amazon's Top 10 Hot New Releases before the book even came out, and the press I had generated through my national interviews, including a mention of the book in *Working Woman Magazine* the month of publication, drove high traffic to the book. I thought it would be a gradual climb but there was quite a bit of excitement before the book even went to print. What a welcome surprise, and strong evidence that before a book, if possible, an author should have a platform. That way there is media buzz and a warm consumer audience for the book when it comes out.

MALONDA RICHARD

Yesterday I was blessed to have an official book release party and everyone who attended had super positive energy. I was even added to the Washington, DC Capitol Bookfest as a panelist because my friend from DC who happened to be in town, came to the event and was impressed with my entire presentation. That friend is a successful author and publisher who has been in the business for a while, and he suggested that I ditch the entire bookstore route and go for maternity wards and anything related to pregnancy.

I went all out for the party and although it was positive, I was disappointed that I only sold about 22 books including 4 that I will receive money for later. I should have listened to my daughter's godmother who told me not to spend more than $50 since she has thrown several book events over the years.

Author of *My Life Isn't Perfect,* Malonda Richard at her NY launch party .

It was frustrating—I know too many people to only have 30-35 guests attend. I spent way too much on the party and could have used that money to pay bills or treat myself to something nice.

I am proud that I did it, but I am going to really figure out how to work this without letting it work me. This is hard work ladies and it is not for the weak or weary. Like I wrote in my blog, writing a book is only one third of the journey. Hopefully you can learn from my experience.

SAMANTHA GIANULIS

If you are an author, writer, or just an impatient person, you do not like seeing "Zero Messages" in Outlook Express or hearing it when you dial your voice mailbox.

In a sales meeting fourteen years ago, my team leader said what was asked of salespeople was tantamount to putting our souls on the chopping block. I never forgot those words—I revisit that sales meeting over and over, in one form or another—promoting my book, querying an editor, convincing my husband to buy me new furniture. All these years later I am still selling, and I have the life-lines on my face to prove it. At my laptop my expression changes from pensive, to desperate, depressed, and less frequently, ecstatic, as I await responses to the pitches I have sent magazines, chefs, newspapers and celebrities.

It's enough to send me into the kitchen at 10:00 am. to cook dinner. That's how I cope—I cook. In the past week I've simmered, slow roasted and sautéed enough food for my neighborhood (I'm on a soup kick right now.)

As I bring the broth to a boil, I glance over at my laptop, sneering at me from the kitchen table. Yes, I have indeed lost my mind, when I think a machine is mocking me.

But at the helm of my stove, adding lentils or peas or risotto, I come back to reality when my rational little voice tells me that never in my life has more patience been required. That's all this is, it's a waiting game. I want my phone to ring off the hook; I want my inbox flooded with messages—just like I want world peace, and enough organic food to feed more people than my neighbors. Just like my five year-old daughter wants to wear lipstick.

Being so closure-driven helped me get my book published, but it handicaps me now, and is one hell of a learning tool when I'm in the mood for personal growth.

I take a deep breath to make sure my soup is accurately seasoned. I have an instinctive feeling that it will work out fine; I'm eccentric enough to believe my obstinacy will expedite fate. Okay, world, humble me—I once heard I can get it in the form of a pie, does that offer still stand? Because I'm awfully hungry.

Nancy Cleary and Christine Hohlbaum (*in from Germany!*) on the way to the
Benjamin Franklin Book Awards, May 31, 2007

MWPC authors meet in New York City at BEA 2007 — *l. to r.* Christine Hohlbaum, Leeda Bacon,
Nancy Cleary, Malonda Richard, Marna Krajeski, Jennifer Kalita.

Pitch your Niche with a Hitch and Get Rich

(I think you can guess which way I pronounce it!)

I want to stress the importance of staying on top of your niche, your specific market, and your genre. You must always keep looking for what's new, and for ways to use this news to your advantage.

How do you do this? Sign up for Google and Yahoo alerts; create a custom Amazon.com home page to alert you of all new book in your genre; join YahooGroups about your topic; subscribe to print magazines in your industry; attend conferences; join professional organizations and visit their websites for upcoming shows often. These are just a few ways to keep on the pulse of new happenings, offerings and trends in your market.

An example of reacting to a current event

Upon hearing the news of a depressed mother drowning her four children, I quickly whisked off a press release to my author whose book helps families coping with a mother's mental illness. What happened the next day could be sheer coincidence, but I believe that because we responded to a current event and offered support to the media, the fish who bit is the biggest fish in the media ocean.

Following is the press release, and the follow-up letter...

Press release I posted on PRWeb.com with same-day distribution.

Wyatt-MacKenzie Publishing, Inc.
DEADWOOD, OREGON

CONTACT:
Nancy Cleary
Wyatt-MacKenzie Publishing
541-964-3314
nancy@wymacpublishing.com

FOR IMMEDIATE RELEASE

Schizophrenic Mother Desperate for "Silent Heroes"

"Silent Heroes"—new award-winning book gives voice and support to all those who have a loved one with schizophrenia or other mental illness

Deadwood, OR - October 21, 2005 - Imagine knowing a mother so desperate, so alone in her struggle, that she commits the horrific act of murdering her three young children. Many friends and families live in silence, they do not seek support or know where to gain comfort for the confusion, loss, and daily struggle of someone with schizophrenia and other mental illnesses. Fearing the bias and stigma long associated with mental illness, namely that somehow the illness is a result of upbringing, poor environment or character weaknesses, they suffer alone.

And yet, they are not alone. One in five Americans over the age of 18 suffers from a mental disorder in a given year, according to the National Institute of Mental Health. Among the American adult population, 2.2 million people have schizophrenia, 18.8 million have a depressive disorder, and 19.1 million have an anxiety disorder. Each of these has a family member, partner or loved ones that are affected by their illness.

In **Silent Heroes Courageous Families Living with Depression and Mental Illness** (Wyatt-MacKenzie Publishing, November 2005; ISBN: 1-932279-18-0) author Maureen Focht reveals the strength and conviction of family members that are usually unrecognized. She provides five key traits of a hero, addresses questions such as: How do we cope? What stages do we go through emotionally and mentally that help us reconcile our commitment? And what are the ways to build resilience?

At age 11, the author watched her mother become a paranoid schizophrenic. Instead of becoming homeless and potentially committing violent crimes, her mother was blessed with a silent hero -the author's father. He remained dedicated throughout the devastating struggle of seeing his beloved wife lose her mind to illness. He exhibited the strength and courage to assist both his wife and children. He is but one example of a hero to celebrate.

Focht is an educator for the Family-to-Family program with the National Alliance for the Mentally Ill, and a training specialist for the nationally known "Parent Project" program and she is on the frontlines for a Public Education Campaign to tell people there is no shame in seeking help. Through her own experiences, and those of other families, she shares the remarkable stories of untold support come from those unseen-family members who have continued to stand by their loved-ones.

Among those you will meet are Norma, Lisa, Les, Christine, and Kevin. Stories of men and women, children, and adults are woven together to offer a complete view of what it is like to witness, be affected by and feel many aspects of the illness of a loved one. Offering the perspective of enlightened witnesses to give voice to feelings unspoken, or even unidentified, provides an initial foundation for support. Partners, siblings and children have little place to turn for encouragement when living with someone with a brain disorder such as schizophrenia, bi-polar, depression or other related illnesses.

Release included tips for the media to share.

W *Wyatt-MacKenzie Publishing, Inc.*
DEADWOOD, OREGON

Schizophrenic Mother Desperate for "Silent Heroes" - page 2 -

From 'Silent Heroes' -resources for friends and families dealing with schizophrenia:

National Institute of Mental Health
www.nimh.nih.gov/healthinformation/schizophreniamenu.cfm

National Schizophrenia Foundation
www.nsfoundation.org

The National Schizophrenia Fellowship, NSF
www.nsf.org.uk

The World Fellowship for Schizophrenia and Allied Disorders
www.world-schizophrenic.org

Schizophrenics Anonymous, SA
www.SAnonymous.org

Named a Finalist Award Winner from USA BookNews 2005 in two categories-Psychology and Social Change, the warmly depicted stories and straightforward approach of this book honors all the silent heroes who remain by the sides of their loved ones.

For more information visit www.theSilentHeroes.com. Contact the publisher for more info on the Mom-Writers Publishing Cooperative and Wyatt-MacKenzie Publishing at www.wymacpublishing.com.

♦♦♦

The next day I got a call from Harpo Studios requesting a review copy! Here's the cover letter I sent with it.

Wyatt-MacKenzie Publishing

The Oprah Winfrey Show
Marci Hughes
110 North Carpenter St.
Chicago, IL 60607

October 22, 2005

Dear Marci,

Per your request I have enclosed an Advance Review copy of our November title "Silent Heroes".

The author is an incredibly compassionate soul whose mission is to remove the stigma of mental illness and thus remove the barriers families face when they desperately need help in coping with a loved one who has depression, schizophrenia, or other mental illness.

The recent events—Tom Cruise's lack of support for the mentally ill, Brooke Shield's wonderful new book, and now, more recently, the poor, poor mom who drowned her three beautiful boys—is a silent scream for silent heroes. I heard a family member say, "She said she was going to go throw the kids to the sharks." Whether they were fearful of the stigma, or they just didn't know how to help, the author and I cried together at the news, knowing her book could heal so many families.

Please contact me if you need any more information.

Warmest Regards,

Nancy

Nancy Cleary
publisher and Mom to Wyatt & MacKenzie

MAUREEN FOCHT

Navigating the Amazon Jungle

March 10 - I sit behind my computer, talking with my webmaster about finalizing my new website, when he mentions that he saw my book on Amazon. I calmly tell him, "That's not possible. My book is not due out until November." He insists he saw my book there. As soon as I get off the phone, I go to the Amazon website. Sure enough, THERE IT IS! And, by golly, they even have it at a discounted price! It is hard to describe my emotions. Excited? Yes, but also upset! How come no one told me it was going on Amazon already? And why is it discounted, already? It's not even out yet! Nancy calmly explains that listings can show up anytime after we provide the distributor the book info (which is 6 months ahead of release!) up until three months prior to publication. She says we have no control over Amazon's pricing logarithm, they do what they wish, and, it does not affect us—this is part of the 55% discount we give the distributor.

I start to calm down and begin wondering how I am going to feel when, in the fall when my book does come out, I see it on Amazon being sold by others at even lower prices. I don't think I will like that.

October 20 - Some of the November releases are already shipping from Amazon, but my book still shows "not released." Oh well, Nancy says wait til November 2, if it still shows that, then we will call.

Oct. 26 - FINALLY! Amazon is shipping my book. But what about these rankings? One day it shows 100,000 something, a couple of days later, it is 800,000 something. This is nuts! How does this work?

October 28 - (Note, only two days later) As I check in with Amazon, my heart almost stops. SOMEONE IS ALREADY SELLING IT FOR A LOWER PRICE! Again, I send an email to Nancy. How can this happen SO FAST? I tell her I just feel like crying. I just don't get it! For my own self-preservation, I realize that maybe this is a good thing. If people are selling it, they must have already bought it.

Nancy tells me these are independent booksellers purchasing through our distributor as well. As I continue to ponder all of this, I realize the issue is one of control. I AM NO LONGER IN CONTROL OF THIS BOOK. It is now "out there." I can no longer worry about how the system and the process works. It is beyond me. I don't know if I will ever understand it.

Getting a Bad Amazon Review

I wish I could say when I read it I thought "whatever."

Since I check my Amazon ranking five times a day,
that made me not want to check anymore.

It really upset me; I took it personal.

Just like I want everyone to like me, I want everyone to like my book.

It was a journey to get to the point where I realized when you put
yourself out to the public, someone is bound to not like you.

I know I have enough people that have given me positive
feedback.

Making the most of Amazon

If I had a dollar for every Amazon question I have received over the last ten years I'd finally be a wealthy publisher! Here are a few of the most asked questions, plus some insider tips.

What does the Amazon discount mean? Do I make less money?

Amazon has an algorithm for their discounts, but these do not affect the royalties you are paid. This discount is taken out of the wholesale discount retailers receive from distributors, usually 55%.

What do the Amazon rankings mean?

I found this chart many years ago and believe it to be surprisingly accurate, at least in responding to the endless requests from authors!

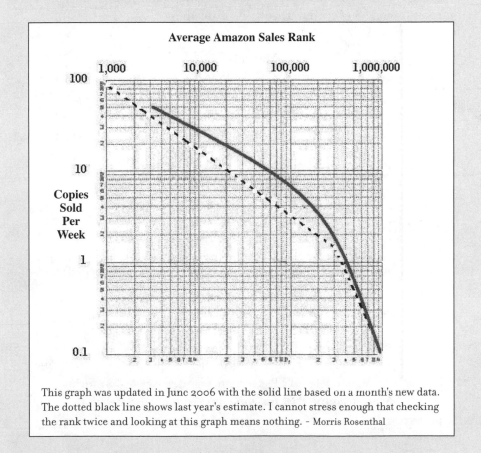

This graph was updated in June 2006 with the solid line based on a month's new data. The dotted black line shows last year's estimate. I cannot stress enough that checking the rank twice and looking at this graph means nothing. - Morris Rosenthal

Who are the people already selling my book? Anyone can sell a copy alongside your listing on Amazon. You can too. Join the "**Amazon Marketplace**" and list yours as "signed by the author." Many of the other links under "available from these retailers" are small independent retailers and online bookstores which purchased through the distributor.

How do I get my books on Amazon? If you do not have distribution in place already (Take our online class to learn more, info on page 187), you can get an "**Amazon Advantage**" account.

If you want to make money linking to books on Amazon from your website or newsletter you can join the "**Amazon Associates**" program which will give you an affiliate code to add to the link and you will be paid a commission on every purchase made through that link.

Amazon Tips

Add content including table of contents, 20-word editorial reviews, excerpt, author bio, and publisher comments. This link has changed over the years. If it does not work check the "Help" section:

http://www.amazon.com/gp/content-form/?ie=UTF8&product=books

Cover Specifications
· TIFF or JPEG format at 72 dots per inch resolution preferred
· A minimum of 500 pixels on the longest side
· RGB color mode
· 8 bits per channel
· File names must consist of the 10-digit ISBN (no dashes needed) e.g., "6004435678.tif" or "1254545332.jpg"
· Image should be a full front view of the cover, with no borders

Cover Submission Detail
All image files must be sent to Amazon using the Internet's FTP (File Transfer Protocol.) For FTP username and password information, email: **image-account-us@amazon.com**. Follow all specifications for preparing and saving documents and images prior to transferring your files.

"Plogs... Amazon Connect and Amazon Daily"— the names and models change often, but the reason is all the same – giving authors the ability to post a blog on their Amazon listing.

Start at www.amazon.com/amazonconnect and click on "Go to Amazon Daily" and then "What is Amazon Daily?" to find all the details.

Amazon Connect is a highly targeted blog where authors can post messages directly to their customers' Amazon.com homepage and to their own product detail pages. By keeping an Amazon Connect blog, authors can communicate easily and directly with an audience of known customers who have purchased their book.

Amazon Connect gives author blogs prime placement on the site by:

- Surfacing an author's posts on their customers' Amazon.com home page.
- Showcasing the three most recent posts by an artist on each of their product pages, directly below the Product Details.
- Posting every message an author writes to their Amazon Connect blog.
- Featuring a link to the author's profile page in a comprehensive Amazon Connect Directory.

Amazon Daily is a blog that contains posts from editors all over the site. Amazon Daily's homepage contains all editorial posts (sorted so the most recent entries appear at the top), and in the side bar you will find Topics where posts are sorted, so you can browse one concept at a time. Each post gives you the opportunity to provide feedback to the sender as to whether you liked the post or not, as well as leave public comments for other customers to see.

Create your own **Amazon Listmania List**—gather all the best books on your topic and create a list and don't forget to include yours. Search Amazon for your topic. On the left side of the listing will appear other Listmania lists and a link "Create a Listmania! list."

Create your own unique **Amazon Bestseller Campaign**. You've probably been on the receiving end of one of these in the last three years—you get an email asking you to buy a book on a certain day to receive a bunch of bonuses. The authors have approached individuals reaching their market (preferably with large email lists) and asked for free giveaways in exchange for the exposure during the campaign and upsell potential to all who purchase. The author and contributors send out their offer to all of their lists a day or so before the designated "Amazon Bestseller Day" and then, in the 24 hours of the campaign, the rankings would rise exponentially. Having outsold many other titles *on that day*, they reach "Amazon Bestseller" status. If may be only fleeting, but its always a great way to spread the news about your book to your market.

Download articles about two Amazon campaigns I helped authors launch: www.wymacpublishing.com/AmazonCampaigns.pdf. In 2003 our own author got to #23, and I helped a colleague get to #8. While these campaigns may be losing popularity, be creative with the model and make your goal to raise awareness about your book and provide your market some benefits instead of trying to become a transient "bestseller."

Launch an Amazon Review Campaign—This is simply a focused effort on getting everyone who purchases your book, or reads in the library, to post an *honest* review on Amazon. Reaching out and asking readers to post truthful reviews, or trading books with a fellow author to post reviews for one another – is not unethical if the reviews are honest and not for the purpose of the reviewers' self-promotion.

Returns—is something wrong with my baby?
A letter from Nancy to the Co-Op

Hi Gals,

I feel a weight. I think it's everyone looking at their sales reports and seeing the high number of returns. You feel as if it is a reflection on your book. I promise you, it is not. The decisions stores make to return books is practically automated; there is no thought behind it. There is nothing wrong with your babies!

Here is a sample of how I can look at the breakdown of your sales. When we get returns, I can see who it was. It also says "hurt" if the book, or whole box of books, has been damaged or signed, or stickered (we learned the hard way)— these are destroyed.

This is a September book—you see the major wholesalers ordering boxes of books in August to have on the store shelves in September. Then, if there are any still in the warehouse or on the shelf when the bill comes due in 90 days, they send them back to our distributor. The return fees and shipping varies, and the freight fee I see every month on the report is painful. But...this is how the big publishers operate.

8/10/2006	BAKER & TAYLOR	SALE	50
8/10/2006	BAKER & TAYLOR	SALE	40
8/15/2006	INGRAM	SALE	30
8/10/2006	BAKER & TAYLOR	SALE	20
8/15/2006	INGRAM	SALE	20
8/10/2006	BAKER & TAYLOR	SALE	10
8/11/2006	BARNES & NOBLE	SALE	2
8/8/2006	AMAZON.COM	SALE	1
8/11/2006	BARNES & NOBLE	SALE	1
8/25/2006	PERSEUS BOOKS	REVIEW	2
- - - - - - - - - - - -			
11/30/2006	AMAZON.COM	SALE	1
11/30/2006	AMAZON.COM	SALE	1
11/7/2006	BAKER & TAYLOR	SALE	1
11/27/2006	BAKER & TAYLOR	RETURN -1	Good
11/10/2006	BAKER & TAYLOR	RETURN -30	Hurt
11/27/2006	BAKER & TAYLOR	RETURN -34	Hurt

Toddlers

Baby's Got Bling!

It's a great feeling to call up a radio producer and have that person book you because they know you're good at what you do. I have gained such an incredible sense of self through the process.

𝒯HE BABY HAS CRAWLED, AND NOW IT toddles—getting into everything possible, tearing it up, and moving on. Unsatiable, never tired, and always loud—a two year-old's characteristics are the requirements for book promotion.

The co-op members share their successes culminating with book award nominations and national TV spots. But do these achievements translate to sales? And what do the Bestseller Lists *really* mean? I'll tell you in Tech Talk.

IN THIS CHAPTER

One Author's Year in Review

Highlights of our Success

Tech Talk – Indie Book Awards

Getting Nominated

Into the Green Room

Tech Talk – Selling Outside of Bookstores

Sales, Expenses & More

PAULA SCHMITT
My First Year in Review

During the month of June I held a book signing at a Barnes and Noble in Burlington, VT. I was so nervous…what if shoppers and my audience didn't like me or my book, or worse yet, what if I didn't sell one book? Luckily, all went well and I made it through the event. And I sold books, imagine that. I also appeared for a book signing at The Dartmouth Bookstore in Hanover, NH.

The month of July was HOT. Not only did I sell some of my books, my name and my book hit several local newspapers and some national ones as well, including *The Chicago Tribune* in a piece about the co-op. I also had fun with more radio interviews. I checked Amazon regularly and I received great reviews. August was busy with book events while I was at Lake Winnipesauke on summer vacation—what a crowd I had. *Living in a Locker Room* also appeared in *The Boston Herald*. I was so excited I thought I would burst. The rest of the month I continued with book events and appeared as a guest on Mom Talk Radio with host Maria Bailey. I was also quoted and mentioned in *Baby and You* magazine.

September was a slower month. I sold a few books and had a book event in Randolph, Vermont in a friendly little book shop. I continued to move forward with my PR agent planning upcoming events and sending out PR to the media.

I can't believe it…*Living in a Locker Room* was named a Finalist Award Winner in USA Book News for "best book" in the humor category. I was shaking and crying so hard. All my hard work actually got noticed. Also in October I was quoted and mentioned in *Family Circle* Magazine, and my online syndicated column, "The All Sports Mom" was given syndication in print with a quarterly column at Kids VT Family Newspaper. Wow.

In November I was quoted in *Parenting* and had a feature article on me in *All You* magazine. I was so excited to be a radio guest in Berkeley, CA with Opal Palmer-Adisa on KPFA FM. They wanted to know all about my Sports Mom role and how I keep it all together. I gave their listeners plenty of advice. I was so happy and proud of my accomplishments.

December was another slow month, I think because of the craziness of the upcoming holidays. My book sold from my website and I was asked to be on WAHM Talk Radio as a guest. And my new internet/podcast radio talk show, Mom Writer's Talk Radio launched.

January 2006 brought many exciting events for me. I was asked to be a Sports Mom Expert at ClubMom. I also was featured in *Hot Moms Club* magazine, *Calgary Child's Magazine* and my syndicated column was added to another magazine in Texas. My book, literary magazine, and radio talk show were in the *Boston Herald* once again.

During February I got a phone call from my PR agent telling me that *NBC Weekend Today* show in NYC wanted me to be a guest on their show about my book! I was so happy and so nervous and just plain shocked. It was arranged and I spent a great weekend in the city and taped my interview with sweaty palms. I also learned that I will be quoted in *Real Simple* magazine spring 2006.

The month of March was a quiet month—not many events though I did sell some books online.

During the month of April I learned that my book was awarded the Parent to Parent Adding Wisdom Award. I also learned that my literary magazine, *Mom Writer's Literary Magazine* was picked by *Writer's Digest* as one of the Best Websites for Writers 2006. I was beaming!

The month of May was exciting. My PR agent called to let me know that she had the attention of *Desperate Housewives* TV star Brenda Strong who wanted to be a guest on my radio talk show, along with bestselling author Jacquelyn Mitchard! I couldn't breathe. I was in shock. Jackie and Brenda were awesome mom writers to chat with and I was only a little bit nervous. Okay, I was so nervous I was drenched with sweat, but the good thing is that no one knew as it was online radio.

Living in a Locker Room is doing wonderful—selling from online retailers and my site. I am one proud mom writer.

Highlights of our Success

CHRISTINE LOUISE HOHLBAUM

It's a great feeling to call up a radio producer and get booked because they know you're good at what you do. I have gained such an incredible sense of self through the process. When people ask me what I really want to do, I tell them I am doing it: writing, doing media relations work, training others to hone their media presentation skills, raising my two children, living in the country and working on new TV show ideas with people who can make it happen.

Christine Louise Hohlbaum's
"Ask Christine" column
in *Hybrid Mom Magazine*.

I'll never forget one experience of having a Disney animator approach me at a beer garden in Munich. When I handed him my book-mark with my book covers on them, his eyes popped open wide, as if he were in the presence of royalty. This from a man who worked on major motion pictures. It is both humbling and gratifying all at once.

Six degrees of separation? That's a book in itself! In my business, there are fewer than six degrees, I believe. *Mom Central* author Stacy DeBroff and I had a great giggle one time about how we were both considered for the same spokesperson position with a national brand cereal company. We didn't know each other at the time, but the subject came up in an online discussion group for women parenting authors, in which we are both members. And at one point, I worked with Stacy's publicist, who had hired me for some PR writing work! Stacy does frequent *Today Show* segments and although my book hasn't been mentioned in such venues yet, I feel an overwhelming sense of joy at watching the process work for other people just like me.

My parenting humor newsletter, "Powerful Families, Powerful Lives", has been running for four years. It is a great way to sustain that style of writing while spreading the word about your own work. It is a useful resource for parents and a chance to give potential readers a flavor for what you do.

I've also launched a CD-Rom, *The Author's Companion: A Self-Guided Course on Book Promotion*, which has been licensed out to various professional publishing organizations. The CD was a natural progression from launching my own book to teaching others how to launch theirs.

JULIE WATSON SMITH

I would receive a call or email from someone in Norway saying she heard about the book project from a friend in Germany who had heard about it from her cousin in France who had heard about it from her sister in New York and so on and so on. It was exciting to see the momentum gained by my one little question of "What did you do today?"

Before the book, I had several mom-inspired programs and workshops. Since the book, I have increased the number of workshops and community groups offered. It's important to remember that you're not just selling a book. You are selling yourself. Think of the book as your accessory. It completes the whole package and gives you a polished, professional image.

MARNA KRAJESKI

Military spouses are a tight group and they have good word of mouth and they are flung out all over the country, so that facilitated publicity. I've gotten emails from readers in Alaska, California, North Carolina, Japan, and Wyoming. Once the book was actually published, my sisters and mother got excited. They bought several dozen copies and handed them out to friends.

I have also launched an e-newsletter called "Household Baggage Bulletin" which I bill as a "grab bag of interesting and useful information for military families." I use the Constant Contact service which is very easy. I think e-newsletters are a great way to get the word out because they can easily be forwarded. Each bulletin has a reference to my book and website.

KATHRYN MAHONEY

I just love getting emails or comments from readers saying they could relate to my stories and were glad they weren't the only ones feeling a certain way about something. And I also love getting emails from people just letting me know that they really enjoyed the book and were going to tell their family and friends about it. I do feel like writing humor is a gift, and I'm glad that people are enjoying this gift. It makes me feel like I have a purpose outside of wiping snotty noses or changing diapers. I can't think of anything better than being able to put a smile on someone's face. Can you?

I try to keep my website updated and fresh; I had an article published in *total180! magazine*; I was featured in *The Lowell Sun* and a Sunday edition of *The Boston Globe*. I'm now working on getting a blog up and running. I submit humorous copy to greeting card companies (and land contracts!) and I continue to write a humor column for my local newspaper.

Kathy Mahoney in *The Boston Globe* and *The Lowell Sun*.

ARLENE SCHUSTEFF

Since my book came out a little over a month ago it has been a whirlwind of activity–quite a wild ride. Silly me, I thought you get your book published and then just sit back and watch it sell. HA! Maybe if you're Mitch Albom or Danielle Steele, but for a first-timer, no way! But perhaps I will be an inspiration to a new writer who thinks that it can't be done. It can–with lots of perseverance and a little bit of luck. I managed to get on *The Greg Behrendt Show* (Okay, full disclosure, I was on for like 40 seconds, but hey, they said the title of the book and it had the title below my face!) and I landed a review in the popular trendy *OK Magazine*. My secret? There was none, I just asked. So if you are reading this and you are scared to take the next step, just do it. (Sorry Nike.) Send out that manuscript, ask for that review, or ask your hubby to watch the kids while you write. Take the first step, the others will follow. Homework, children, and chicken nuggets call.

Arlene Schusteff gets local and national media.

IRIS WAICHLER

There have been so many highlights so far. I got a phone call from the founder of the Mom's Radio Network. She does a radio show using contributed telecasts from many experts. She asked me to be a regular contributor as their infertility expert. I also got a phone call from a marketing executive in New York. She had a client who was promoting a wonderful infertility product. They were looking for somebody who had personal infertility experience and had written a book on the subject. She asked if I would be their spokesperson as an infertility expert, and they are in the midst of designing a national radio and TV campaign which she has asked me to participate in. Amazingly both of these offers came from people who did not know me but found me through my website. The book has taken me in challenging yet fun directions I had not imagined before.

I got an email from someone about a teleconference. I signed up and then the woman who led the teleconference gave me a tip about a reporter doing an article that I might contribute to. I wrote the reporter who was very excited to hear from me and used my comments and plugged my book in the article. It got me national exposure.

The radio program and this national marketing campaign are major ways I am hoping will promote the book. I have written articles for RESOLVE, the national infertility organization that had given me extra visibility. I also do educational/workshop programming for them as well. I wrote another article for a large magazine that has a readership of 400,000 and that gave me some great exposure. I also have tapped into the Internet and have done some author interviews there to increase my visibility. As a result of a teleconference I learned about a woman who is an expert at marketing and making pitches to advertise your product. She has a list of 5000 national radio, TV, and print media people to contact in specific specialty markets. I am excited about this. She has had an incredible success rate.

NINA MARIE DURAN

The most memorable media highlight for me was when I did a radio show and the host said, "Okay callers number 9 and 10 will get an autographed book." I'll never forget the feeling of seeing all of the lines ringing. There were 19 lines and they were all lit up! I thought, "Oh my

God they're blinking for me!" I never really took in all of it until I lay down that night. I was so thankful for what I have.

TERILEE HARRISON

For me, it wasn't, "Oh, I got on a huge TV show." Instead I'm constantly going out there and networking; going to women's expos and having opportunities to meet hundreds of women in a day. So for me it was seeing the women face to face and hearing the women say, "Oh I need this and my sister needs it too." If they bought one, they usually bought two. It's all about looking them in the eye and knowing that I was helping them.

The media comes every day. I just got an email today that AT&T is quoting me in an article. It's a steady stream. It's something you always have to be open to —you never know where the next call is going to come from. Don't be disappointed if you're scheduled for a certain show and it gets cancelled, just move on to the next one.

CHRISTIE GLASCOE CROWDER

Last night I was on a live local radio show called "Teen Talk." The hostesses were two lovely young ladies, seniors in high school who were voracious for information about the college experience. We talked before the show, during commercial breaks, and after the show. It was great! We talked about everything...sororities, parties, safety, health, homesickness...you name it. And it was (of course) great publicity for the book but what really excited me was that I really felt that I made a difference to these girls (and to their audience of 20,000+). They were wide-eyed and attentive to everything I had to say. I actually felt like an "expert" for the first time in this whole process. It was a relaxed conversation as if they were my little sisters asking me to tell them the stories of my youth, which is *exactly* what I am going for. If I ever had any doubts about my book and my message and my ability to do some good in this world...they all disappeared in that one happy little hour on Radio Sandy Springs.

MAUREEN FOCHT

I was on a cruise ship and sure enough, that's when *Oprah* requested a review copy! So there I was, on a cruise, monitoring my time on the

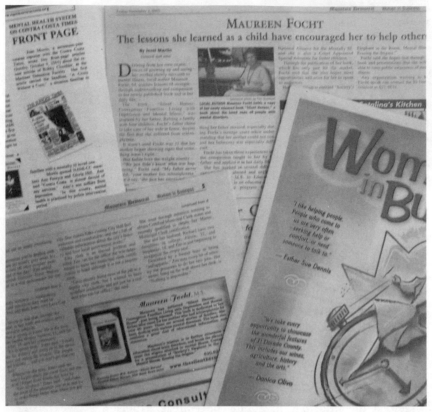

Maureen Focht gets local and national media for *Silent Heroes*.

computer because I have to pay for every minute, trying to communicate with my publisher and my publicist. I knew—okay, they asked for the book, but is anything going to happen? It didn't, but I am still hopeful!

It was so very gratifying to have top professionals in the book business validate my work. *Silent Heroes: Courageous Families Living with Depression and Mental Illness* was a winner in the "Social Change" category of USA Book Awards and was a winner in the the National Indie Excellence 2007 Book Awards!

PAMELA JO LEO

Because I don't have a college degree, and am an independent scholar, getting my hero Joseph Chilton Pearce's endorsement was like getting my Ph.D. in human development. Personally and professionally I knew what kind of doors that would open for me; I knew that people in my field would say if that's what he thinks of her work, then we need to look at it.

I was beyond thrilled when I heard how excited Nancy was about my book *Connection Parenting* being a finalist for a *ForeWord Magazine* Book-of-the-Year Award. I am so proud to be part of the mom writers co-op and so grateful to have Nancy as my publisher. Part of my joy in this news is that it made her so happy, another part of is that it's a win for all of us. When Wyatt-MacKenzie gets recognition, we all win.

I called my mom, I called my daughters, and did the happy dance with my three grandchildren. They were all here seeing the four new baby goats when I got the call from Nancy. They were definitely more excited about the goats than Gramma's news but they happy danced with me just because I was so happy.

I was always confident that the content of my book was exceptional but being a finalist (and losing to a book from the American Academy of Pediatrics) made me feel that my writing was exceptional too. For a writer without a college degree that means a lot to me.

Pam Leo gets local and national media for *Connection Parenting*.

Indie Book Awards

Benjamin Franklin Awards
$75 per entry
www.pma-online.org
DEADLINE Dec. 31

ForeWord Magazine Book-of-the-Year
$70 per entry
www.forewordmagazine.net/awards/
DEADLINE Jan.15

The Nautilus Awards
$125 per entry
www.independentpublisher.com/nautilus/
DEADLINE Feb. 15

The National "Indie Excellence 2008" Book Awards
$49 per entry
www.pubinsider.com/indieexcellenceawards.html
DEADLINE March 31

IPPY
Independent Book Awards
$70 per entry
www.independentpublisher.com/ipland/v4/IPAwards.htm
DEADLINE April 1

National BEST BOOKS Awards
USA Book News Best Book Award
$49 per entry
www.usabooknews.com
DEADLINE August 31

NAPPA National Parenting Publications Awards competition
$65 per entry
www.nappa.parenthood.com or call NAPPA at 617-522-1515 x23
DEADLINE September 1

IRIS WAICHLER
Getting nominated...

As you read *A Book is Born* it becomes clear that your book is "your baby." We all want everyone to like our children. We want people to think they are smart, funny, and good looking. We want them to see what kind of contribution our children make in the world. Deep down we know that on many levels our "children" are an extension of us. They are a part of us and we create and shape them. Consequently we want our "children" to be liked and we also want to be liked. It is human nature.

I learned this week that I received a national award saying that my book was best of the year in its category. The email said "Congratulations, you are a winner...." The next day I got another email and it said "Congratulations, you have been chosen by our judges to be a finalist for the best book of the year award." I thought, "Why are they sending me another announcement?" Then I looked at it more closely and realized this was a different award.

I was shocked by the first award and stunned at the second. I admit I jumped up in the air and pumped my fists and did a ridiculous little dance that in retrospect I was grateful nobody else saw. Oh yes, I forgot to mention the large WOO WOO cheer I let out that caused my husband to come see what had happened to make me go off the deep end. I got congratulatory kisses from my husband and my 6 year-old daughter. By the way, this all happened a couple of days before the Oscars. All I had been hearing over the last weeks was talk about awards, how it feels to be nominated, and does it or doesn't it matter if you win? I agonized about whether to even enter the first competition that I ended up winning. I wasn't sure my book would fit the criteria. It costs money each time you enter. All of the above got me thinking about awards and how I really feel about them.

My first thought was of course I love to win awards! Who doesn't? What better feeling is there than having people who have some expertise, influence in the book industry, and no personal agenda, tell you that your book is excellent? It gave me a great deal of personal satisfaction to know that my work received the approval of these judges. It was my Sally Field moment—"You like me, you really like me." (You may have guessed I am a huge Oscar fan.) There is a different meaning for me when judges give my book a positive critique as opposed to my family and friends. Both feel really good and I am incredibly grateful for whatever kind words people are willing to bestow on my "baby" and me. But awards are a public forum with far reaching consequences. I had not been on Amazon lately because I got tired of watching my ranking sink in a zone below the million mark. My curiosity got the best of me and I looked and with delight saw my ranking had immediately jumped above 100,000. This occurred the day I sent my press release about my award out. That's what I call a fabulous consequence.

I love to be nominated for awards too. The message to me is the same—"we saw something special in your book and we want to publicly acknowledge it." A nomination is public recognition. I have never been one of those people who have to win, so nominations feel great too.

Why do I enter awards competitions? It is difficult and anxiety-provoking to put yourself and your "baby" out there to be examined so closely and publicly. In my heart I do it because it feels good when the nominations and awards go my way. Another important aspect is awards and nominations ensure that my book will be seen by more people. That is part of why I write. I want to reach as many people as I possibly can with my message. I want everyone to read my "baby." We all know an Oscar guarantees a larger box office and a longer, wider run in the movie theatres. These book awards and nominations mean higher book sales, greater exposure, and maybe if you are really lucky a longer shelf life.

I wish you luck with the labor and birth of your "baby." I hope that you will someday read the words "Congratulations you are a winner …"

Into the Green Room — Baby Gets a Khyron!

Arlene Schusteff gets a khyron (the graphic on the bottom
of the screen) on *The Greg Berhendt Show*

ARLENE SCHUSTEFF

You go through all this effort and you put yourself out there in so many
different arenas, and the things you think are going to really come
through and happen, don't. Then other surprising things just sort of pop
up. One of those, my biggest national success, was *The Greg Berhendt
Show*. That was one of those things when you just needed to be at the
right place at the right time. I was on Craigslist looking for furniture and
I ventured over to the TV section. I'm still not sure what made me go over
there. I was scrolling down and it read, "Do you want to be on a TV talk
show? Do you have an interesting story to tell?" So I sent the publicist a
book, a press release, and a letter pitching me and the book. Then I
forgot about it. Six weeks later, a producer from the show left me a voicemail. I listened to it three times, because I thought I was imagining it.
She said she just wanted to talk to me. The problem was, by the time I
heard the message, it was 10:00 at night. So I had this whole evening of
anticipating and wondering. That night I watched "Sex and the City"
when Carrie has her booksigning, and I saw that as a sign!

The next morning I called the producer and she told me they were
casting a show about "women that were too tired to have sex with their
husbands." She asked me if I was too tired to have sex with my husband
and I thought, "Honey, I can be anything you want me to be, just get me
on TV with the name of my book!" So, while I was silently apologizing to
my husband, I told her yes, I was definitely one of those women. She said

she read the book, and I sounded great, but she wanted to "save" me for another show. At the time I thought it was a major blow off, thinking she'd never call me. But she promised to keep in touch and we hung up.

I was disappointed, and really glad I hadn't told anybody. Then, about a month later, on my caller ID, there she was again. So I called her back. This time she was casting a show on extreme parenting. She wanted me to come on and be the voice of reason.

Five days later I was on a plane to LA—me, my book, and my friend. She had asked if I had any friends willing to do some pre-tape segments. Of course I had a million friends who wanted to go with me. We just could not believe this was happening. It seemed surreal.

I got to LA and rode a limo to the hotel. The next day we were picked up by a big van with the *The Greg Behrendt Show* logo on the side. Our driver was fresh out of college and told us stories of some of the celebrities that had already appeared on the show. Then, just like in the movies, we pulled up to the big studio gate and it opened. While we were driving through the lot the driver pointed out where the shows *Las Vegas* and *Deal or No Deal* were filmed. We saw a bunch of the *Deal or No Deal* models walking around! We felt like celebrities.

When we got there, an assistant producer met us and walked us to our dressing room, which had both of our names on it! She told us we could go in there and relax and someone would be with us soon. We were in shock.

They brought us lunch and talked about how they wanted us to act on camera. Then they brought us to hair and makeup, which was probably the funniest part of the day. Not only were we getting our hair and makeup done, the hairdresser had just finished doing the *Extreme Makeover* people and gave us the inside scoop.

We were sitting in our dressing room when we heard a commotion outside. We peeked out and saw Tia Carerra from *Wayne's World*, who was also appearing on the show. We said hello, she said hello, and we closed the door and did a silent scream mouthing "OH MY GOD!"

The assistant producer then brought us behind the stage and put mikes on us, snaking them up our shirts, and walked us to the front row of seats. The rest of the audience were already seated, looking at us like "Who are these people?"

Greg came out and the show started rolling. The assistant producer told me Greg would come to me after the break. As soon as the commercial break started the hairdresser came running up to me, and then the makeup artist; they poofed me and powdered me, and instructed me to not put my hair behind my ears.

We came back from the break and Greg mentioned my name and the name of my book and I thought "Okay, I can die now." I stood up and we had a five minute dialogue on the book and parenting and motherhood. I couldn't tell you now for the life of me what I said, but the crowd was cheering so I know I resonated with them. When I sat back down my friend said, "Oh my God, who knew you had this in you, you were a natural!" I sat through the rest of the show half in panic he was going to talk to me again and half in disbelief that I was even there.

After the show the producer came up to me to take the mike off and she said, "You were absolutely fabulous, we'll definitely have you back again." We waltzed back up to the dressing room to get our stuff and there was a knock on the door. Greg gave me a big hug and said "You were great, I just want to say thank you." And we took a couple of pictures.

On the way back to the hotel I still felt surreal. I kept thinking, "I was just on national TV. My name was on national TV. Did this really happen?" Then two months later when the show aired—I was assured that yes, it did. We didn't know what day it was going to air, we were told one date and then it actually aired one week sooner so I had about five minutes to call my family and friends and tell them to watch me.

I watched it, looking to see what I looked like, not listening to what I said. It really hit me for the first time that I was an author when under my face on the screen it said "Author, *Peanut Butter, Playdates and Prozac*". Nothing until that moment made it sink in until I actually saw it on TV. Nothing drove it home like that did.

Samantha Gianulis gets a khyron on *iVillage LIVE*

SAMANTHA GIANLUIS

Okay, here I was dicing ginger for the salsa, with the brand new Calphalon knives iVillage just received. No sooner did the producer say, "Those are really sharp!" than I sliced off top of my middle finger. But even Mario Batali and Bobby Flay did that, and it was Friday the 13th, so I considered it good luck even though it set us behind. Then the wind blew (it was a semi-outdoors pavilion type sound stage) and my flames didn't get high enough to cook the quesadilla quickly enough. But thanks to the magic of television, this was minimized and we had everything done before the guests started to trickle in. I wasn't worried about chatting with the host. I just wanted to represent myself as a worthy cook. Every time a self-sabotaging thought came into my head, such as "You're out of your league," or "You're going to fall flat on your face," I shooed it away and moved right on. Getting the bleeding under control and letting the sous chef do most of my prep work was the hardest part.

Afterwards, the producer told me to keep in touch, hopefully a good sign. I don't know. What I do know is that I am so freaking glad it's over! I was so proud to be up there representing Wyatt-MacKenzie and all of us. I wasn't up there alone. I had my family, God, my friends, MWPC and MWLM (*Mom Writer's Literary Magazine*) with me. I wasn't nervous. Humility has a place in all of my conversations but I knew it would be okay, I just knew. And when things went wrong—cutting off a good chunk of my middle finger, an underachieving burner to cook food on live TV—I smiled and told myself that now those things were out of the way I could relax. As the live segment ticked second by second on, it felt like I had brought my A-game and secured a win.

Now I'm in my hotel room in Orlando two days after filming my television debut. I can't believe all of this. I used to feel that I didn't deserve good fortune, but you know what? Why should I begrudge what the Universe gives me, or scoff at the laws of attraction? There are things going on much bigger than me. I'm only a small part but my little life just became way more public not only through my book, but my appearance in front of many...and I am okay with that. I LOVE what I am part of...Wyatt Mackenzie Publishing, *Mom Writer's Literary Magazine*, and Family Food Network. I am PROUD of what I've done and those who read this will understand. Reaching a goal and feeling you've earned it—feeling secure that you can take care of those you love by what you do is a beautiful feeling and I wish it for everyone.

The television promotion of my book is over. My finger still hurts, but the support I got dulls the pain. I hoped I would do well. I risked humiliation, but overall, I tried to compose myself with what I know, and who I am thus far. I'm flying back to San Diego with peace of mind and a little more spring in my step.

My kids are telling me it's time for bed. I could write all night but it'll have to wait. It's okay though, because these stories stay in my mind; they sometimes write themselves—and more importantly, keep me standing on solid ground where I am not afraid to look behind or ahead. I can see pretty far...especially in my dreams. So goodnight.

LEEDA BACON

Oh my gosh, I just did my first TV interview! What fun! I wasn't nervous at all. This has been a very busy month and it is just getting started. BEA in NY was a great time and it was wonderful to meet those of you who were able to attend. We all are so diverse yet we have so much in common. I learned a lot from that trip, making it well worth the expense. I'll be doing a seminar on Monday for The California Department of Food and Agriculture, which I'm a bit scared about. My official book signing is June 18 at the office of the doctor who endorsed the book. He is catering it! Then I fly to North Carolina where I'll do another TV spot and a book signing. If you pick up an *All You* magazine, you'll see a tiny

Leeda Bacon gets a khyron on *The Good Morning Show* in North Carolina

article about me (the phone interview I did with them was quite long, so I was surprised by the shortness of the article.) I just received an email from a prominent doctor who specializes in heart disease and diet and he wants to review my book! I'm sending it out today.

I share this because I know all of you have experienced the same amazing things when your book first came out. I've learned from you that the momentum slows down after awhile, but right now I'm riding the wave. As always, many thanks to all of you for your advice and comments. *Be Ye Encouraged*—TV is easy! You can do it!

CHRISTIE GLASCOE CROWDER

I landed this great media by being persistent. I emailed the show's producer with a "graduation" themed pitch about a month after the book was released. I really did not expect a reply right away so you will imagine my shock when I received a response in less than 30 minutes. She asked for a copy of the book, which I happily sent her along with a media kit. I waited about two weeks then sent her a follow up email. No response for about a month. Graduation season was about at it's end, at least in Georgia. Here, the school year is over before Mother's Day. I was getting disappointed but not discouraged. I had another shot, a "back-to-school" pitch. It's not as strong as graduation (you don't really get gifts for going to school), but it was still a sellable angle. I pitched her again for back to school. Silence. I was about to give up when I received a message from her saying that she had not forgot about me and they are working on back-to-school segments and I should hear from her soon.

Then again, silence. I could hear crickets chirping. I decided at that moment to just let it go and concentrate on other things... like my upcoming book signing event. I sent out my newsletter and my invitation to all of my local friends and contacts...including the *Good Day Atlanta* producer. Two days later, I receive this message: *Hey Christie, I got your latest information. I saw that you were having a book signing next Saturday, August 4th. Would you be available to come on Good Day on Wednesday, August 1st in the 7am hour?*

If there was a bigger grin than the one of the famed Cheshire Cat, I was wearing it! My 2 month-old son Jackson was sound asleep in the bassinet next to me so I couldn't scream like I wanted to. My elation ("I'm going to be on TV!") quickly turned to panic ("Oh no, I'm going to be on TV!"). I have no clothes that fit. It's either maternity or my husband's too-small sweats...neither of which will do. My hair is a mess, I am sporting an Eddie Munster uni-brow, and I refuse to go on TV with glasses which means new contacts are in order. Operation "Christie's TV Make-over" was in full effect. Two potential outfits, a hairdo, a manicure/pedicure, new contact lenses (and too much money spent) later, I was ready for my close-up. I began to brood over what I planned to say for my three minutes of fame. I wanted to talk about my sister, get my book message out, mention *A Book Is Born*, and if there was time, get in a little blurb about life coaching... yes, I was planning to do all of that in three minutes!

The day of the show came and to my surprise, I was not that nervous. The staff was really wonderful and made me feel at home. My husband Curtis and (almost) 3 year-old daughter Kennedy tagged along to cheer me on. Kennedy was her usual cute self and really hammed it up with the staff and other guests. She really enjoyed seeing me get my make up done. Then it was show time! Lights, camera, action! It was over in a flash. It went so fast I cannot even remember what I said or how I sounded when I said it. When we cut to commercial, Suchita beamed with excitement telling me how great I did. She couldn't believe this was my first live appearance. So, I guess that means it went well.

Like I said, it was only a three-minute segment so I was not able to get much in. We mostly covered my inspiration for the book and how it is really timely for young girls today. No such luck for the latter two talking points on my list... I mean, I did have to let Suchita (the hostess) talk too, right? The good thing is I now have a great relationship with the

Christie Crowder gets a khyron on *Good Day Atlanta*

producers and hosts thanks to my 3 year-old "publicist," Kennedy. She charmed the pants off of everyone at the station. They want her to come back and visit so there is my "in" for *A Book Is Born* (and other YBS Guides) in the future. Note to any of you planning to promote on TV, take cute kids to the green room! I have not watched the interview yet. All who saw it live and online said I did well and looked great. I am a little skeptical...not exactly thrilled that my television debut was with loads of post-baby weight, but all in all, it felt great.

The morning after, I checked my website traffic...it had quadrupled in the past 24 hours. The book signing on Saturday was mentioned on the show at the end of my interview so I am looking forward to a great turnout.

So the net of it is...be persistent. The producer told me that she never received so much "follow up" from a guest in her life. I'll take that as a compliment!

IRIS WAICHLER

My Dream Came True, not Once but Twice last week…

I remember the first day I began to write my book. It was about five years ago and I had just started my research to see if I even wanted to pursue my book project. Did I have something new or different to say? I decided that I had something to add to the body of work already out there on infertility related issues. I put down my pen and closed my eyes. I just sat there a moment imagining what would be the most personally gratifying response I could get on my book. I didn't think about awards, which I couldn't even imagine. Making money wasn't in my realm of thinking either. (My personal money goal was to break even.) I imagined receiving a letter from somebody struggling with infertility, what it would say, and how my book might have impacted the reader.

∽✲∾

My dream came true not once but twice in the last couple of weeks. I received an email from a woman who had an incredibly painful infertility journey. She had been distraught and feeling hopeless. This was her last chance at becoming a parent. She had bought my book months ago but hadn't read it. In desperation she picked up my book and described how she read through the night and cried as she read it because it helped her feel less alone, it gave her hope, and it told her how to cope with some of the people and issues she had been struggling with. She attached a letter she had written to her family. She was empowered in the midst of her sadness. She had gotten the courage to write the letter from reading my book. She explained after she read it she called her doctor's office to explain to them what she needed from them. I cried as I read her letter because it was the letter I had dreamed of. The best part was the next day she wrote to tell me she was pregnant. I confess I cried again for her joy and the fact that she shared it with me.

The next week I co-led a workshop on infertility with a couple who had read my book. We had not met. They started the workshop by saying that they were thrilled to read a book where "somebody gets it—she really gets and writes about what we are going through." They advised the participants to read my book to feel less alone and learn how to cope. I was living my dream again. It felt wonderful and gratifying. I love a happy ending!

Sales, Expenses & More

I asked the co-op members to share their thoughts on sales and expenses. I've included a few of their responses here anonymously, with two sample income/expense reports.

Sales are okay, but could be better. But I know the reason they're not great is because I haven't put the effort into the sales process like I should. I found that being a mom and an author simultaneously is pretty crazy and my stress tolerance ain't the best. So...family comes first, which means the book has to come second and sales have suffered.

Writing a book—does it make cents? "How many will you have to sell to recoup your investment?" asked one of my well-meaning friends after I explained my vision. Annoyed, I said, "A lot." My friend just doesn't get it.

Book sales are not the only way to make money on your book. In fact, if they were, how would you even measure when you broke even—given all the blood, sweat, tears, and life experience that go into writing and publishing a book?

In fact, I've heard that writing a book is just a door opener to a public speaking career. I never knew I wanted to be a public speaker, I certainly don't feel ready right now, at this moment. But that doesn't mean I won't be in a year, five years, or ten years...or tomorrow.

All the work I have done, and continue to do, builds the foundation for future success of unknown magnitude. That is the hope I hold in my heart, and the motivation that keeps me moving on, sometimes just a step at a time, and sometimes a step backward, but always facing forward.

There were days when I said to myself, "Why am I doing this?" It was an overwhelming process, but in the end, totally worthwhile. I learned a lot about the publishing industry and I also learned a lot about myself. I learned that I really enjoy writing, but am not really interested in, nor good at, sales. This is the reason my book isn't on the NY Times bestseller list, or any other list for that matter! But I also learned that my real goals were to be able to document my family's stories, have some of the proceeds of the book go to the American Diabetes Association because my brother and sister both suffer from this disease, and to dedicate the book to my grandmother, who passed away a few years ago. When I realized that by just publishing the book, I had achieved all of these things, I started to relax a little and realized that any sale is a good sale.

⌒

It is tough to know exactly how sales are at this time, I am nearing the end of the 1st quarter. It is going okay. I don't have much to compare it with. I still feel a strong need to hustle and get the word out there about the book. Marketing and sales remain important goals for me now on a daily basis. I try to come up with new ideas to work on increasing my sales. I hope the numbers will climb with time.

⌒

Food for thought: I think if you asked 100 authors their thoughts on this topic you could get 100 different answers. New authors need to be aware of the expenses that are ahead. While it is fulfilling, publishing a book can also be extremely frustrating. You enter into it not knowing exactly how much money it actually takes to get your book out there. For me, I like to know every fact and every detail so that I can go into things with my eyes wide open. Being fully aware of the expense of actually publishing a book and marketing it may deter new authors but at least they can be fully informed so that they can plan ahead. Knowledge is power.

⌒

I can't really give a breakdown as to how much money I have put into my book. In the beginning it was an issue, now I'm just glad I did it. Sometimes losing control (even of finances) can mean finding something greater.

And when you don't have enough resources, it forces you to be creative. When you want something, you make it happen. Is that not the truth? The last thing I want to do is scare off a new author with numbers. They can be intimidating and I would hate for someone to miss out on all the joys of publishing because of finances. My advice is this: "If you want it, do it." Make it happen.

Income/Expense Reports

Example Author #1 First Year Book Expenses & Income:

Classes/Writing Conferences $1,500 (Erma Bombeck Conference)
Professional Editing $0 (family member did it for free)
Marketing Package $500
Printing 2500 Bookmarks $200
Illustration for book $300
Photo for book $75
Online hosting $100/year
Web design $0 (friend did it for free and I update it)
200 Books to sell myself, with shipping $1,000
PR $0 (emailed press releases everywhere)
Advertising $0 (free through online newsletter)
Travel $0 (included in conference price above)

Income from books I sold plus royalties $2300
Other income from writing gigs $300

Example Author #2 First Year Book Expenses & Income:

Writing:
   Editing: $300
   Illustration: $350
Publishing and Marketing expenses:
   Marketing & Author Branding Package $950
   Printing posters for author events $10
   Printing press releases and sell sheets $15
   Website Hosting and Domain $250
   PR $250
   Mailing of ARCs and books to prospective reviewers $125
   Book Conference, flight $130, hotel $400

Royalty income and book sales $1400
Article income $250

Selling Outside of Bookstores

You will hear the experts tell you over and over to think outside the bookstore when selling your books, and truly, the only major bucks come from making large quantity sales.

First a quick note about **Rights Sales**, which are wonderful gems of hidden profit. Selling the publication rights to a large publishing house, licensing foreign and translation rights, granting book club rights, and selling audio and performance rights—could all be potential gold mines.

Where the money is...

When you can match your book with a group of people who need it and a corporation which has the money to pay for them (and benefit immensely from the positive social publicity they receive) you have a win/win/win.

On page 161 is an example of a **Private Label Package**. We matched up a beautiful book written by a young mom about embracing your child, with a parenting support organization. Our goal was to private label a print run with their logo on the cover and information about the organization on the back, to be distributed to young women nationwide through their organization paid for by grants. Notice the steep discounts a corporation will expect for a large quantity order, up to 90%, but when you see the size of the profit, you have to appreciate these large, one-shot sales!

Alternative Fundraising

On the following page is an example of "Sponsorship Packages" – an idea for authors to raise money for their expenses by selling sponsorship in their books and media.

Sponsorship Flyer

NINA   MARIE   DURAN

author ·········· *speaker* ·········· *spokeswoman* ·········· *empowered mom*

Elijah on My Mind Sponsorship Levels

36 Color Sponsorship: $2500 and over
- Acknowledgements inside each copy of *Elijah on My Mind*
- Mentioned at each book signing, radio and television appearance
- Logo/name will be printed on event materials
- Acknowledgement in press releases
- Logo/Name on banners displayed at every book event, private parties, book signings, and seminars

24 Color Sponsorship: over $1200 - $2400
- Acknowledgements inside each copy of *Elijah on My Mind*
- Mentioned at each book signing, radio and television appearance
- Logo/name will be printed on event materials

12 Color Sponsorship: over $500 - $1200
- Acknowledgements inside each copy of *Elijah on My Mind*
- Logo/Name mentioned at collection of events, private parties, book signings, and seminars.

8 Color Sponsorship: $100 - $500
- Acknowledgements inside each copy of *Elijah on My Mind*

13614 Barsan Road, San Antonio TX, 78249   PH: 210.643.4288

w w w . n i n a m a r i e d u r a n . c o m

Private-Label Flyer

N I N A   M A R I E   D U R A N

Nina Marie Duran's book *Elijah on My Mind* retails for $12.00 and will be released September 1, 2006

PRE-PUBLICATION CUSTOM LABELING PACKAGE

Custom Package will include the following:
- add your logo and/or slogan to FRONT COVER
- add logo and information on the BACK COVER
- preparation of all artwork, print handling

ORDER SIZE	DISCOUNT	COST	Shipping Estimate to TX
5,000	70%	$3.60 each	$500.00
10,000	80%	$2.40 each	$750.00
20,000	85%	$1.80 each	$1000.00
50,000	90%	$1.20 each	$1750.00

TERMS are 50% down with Purchase Order by June 5, 2006 – paper order will be placed June 5.
BALANCE open approval of Proof of final cover July 15, 2006
SHIPPING costs will be determined once books ship, payable by August 15, 2006

BOOKS will ship on or about August 1, 2006, expect delivery by August 15, 2006.

Any questions can be directed to publisher, Nancy Cleary, at 541-964-3314 or nancy@wymacpublishing.com

Wyatt-MacKenzie Publishing, Inc.
DEADWOOD, OREGON

NANCY C. CLEARY
The "BS" in Bestseller Lists

How does a book get on the "Bestseller" lists?

Well, we've learned to get on Amazon's "Bestseller" list by running an "Amazon Campaign" offering downloadable goodies to every customer who buys from Amazon within a 24-hour period. Randy Gilbert was the originator of the craze in 2003 (*see page 130*.)

We've also learned you can get on the "Amazon Bestselling New Releases" list when a major distributor places a large Amazon *preorder* for the shelves when the title is hyped for big media. I didn't realize Amazon could also return books until watching one author get national media garnering a large Amazon order, only to have a large percentage returned in 60 days (to be reordered later, of course.)

And, speaking of large distributor orders, *THAT* is how to get your book on the big Bestseller Lists. In order to be counted, the orders have to go through the book system—processed by a major book distributor. When the major publishing houses present their titles 6 months in advance of the publication date, they are also presenting their $100,000+ marketing budgets—and the distributor places orders accordingly. It all goes hand in hand. The authors you see doing the "circuit" of all the news and talk shows, and whose books you see on the endcaps of bookstores in the mall, those are the ones also appearing on the Bestseller Lists because those are the ones with the most money and hype AND (here's the clincher) these *preorders* can also be returned which does NOT count against the sales and does not remove the book from the previous month's Bestseller List. (Get my point?) Some best-sellers aren't even really sold to the end customer, they only travel through the distribution machine and those numbers counted.

Of course the exceptions are the perennial sellers that appear on the list for weeks, even years on end, many of which (but not all) were originally launched with a media blitz and the ripples are still rolling outward.

Are there runaway bestsellers? Of course. There are *a few* wonderful stories of successful authors from independent houses, even those who've self-published, that have gone on to bestseller status.

CHAPTER 7

Raising Books & Babies

The Life of a Mom Writer

*W*E FORGET THE PAIN OF CHILDBIRTH and go on to have more children—to play with our first, to multiply our efforts (if you're cooking for 3 might as well cook for 5 or 6...) and to add to our legacy.

I asked the co-op members if they planned on expanding their family with future books and other projects, and they discussed the influence publishing has had on their life.

Tech Tips has the best advice, resources and tips we have to share.

"Becoming a published author reaffirms that I can reach any goal I set. Reaching and exceeding my goals will affect my children's lives. It encourages them to find and do what makes them happy."

IN THIS CHAPTER

More Babies

How having a book has changed our lives

Tech Tips

Our Favorite Resources & Tips for Mom Writers

More babies? How has your book influenced your life?

IRIS WAICHLER

I have been doing a number of articles relating to topics from my book. I am also enjoying my radio work and would like to do more of that if possible. I am still hoping to get some television exposure. Aside from contributing to *A Book is Born*, I don't plan on starting another writing project.

I am in the early stages of promoting my book, just the fourth month since it was published. Being a published author has been extremely useful as I have approached people to do articles and speaking engagements. Reviews and interviews I did on the internet have been surprisingly fruitful in terms of people learning about me and contacting me. The Internet is a hugely important tool in this whole process.

I see these events as useful tools to get local and national exposure for my book so I generally am not charging for these projects right now. I view them as important marketing vehicles that will eventually make me more money. However, I did earn some money on an article I wrote.

I view getting my book published as a real accomplishment in today's competitive publishing market. Seeing my book on Amazon, in newspapers and magazine articles, and bookstore windows has been enormously satisfying. People coming to me for advice and information, and contributing to media events has also felt great.

The reason I wrote my book was to help others struggling with infertility, and by far the most gratifying part of this process has been the communications I've received from people coping with it. Achieving this goal has been my proudest accomplishment to date in relation to my book project. I believe people now perceive me as having expertise in this area and I am certain I will continue with writing, speaking, and media endeavors offering information to help this population. It feels like a natural offshoot from my counseling and social work experience.

These new challenges and opportunities are very exciting for me and the possibility of reaching more people in new places is really great. My book is being sold in other countries, places I never dreamed would be possible. My 6 year-old daughter knows I am doing author events and writing articles. She was photographed for one of the articles. She asked me, "How long before you are really famous, Mama?" I am not quite sure how to respond to that question. I just tell her I am hoping it will happen soon.

JULIE WATSON SMITH

I have two more books I'm working on. I also offer a series of workshops for moms and am currently developing after-school programs for kids. Additionally, our product line includes the *Chaos Companion*, a mom-inspired dayplanner.

The revenue stream has started to trickle. I look forward to the day when it floods.

Becoming an author reaffirms that I can reach any goal I set. Reaching and exceeding my goals by becoming a published author and entrepreneur will affect my children's lives. It encourages them to find and do what makes them happy. As for my readers, I'm happy to say that I've received such positive feedback about how they feel connected to each other. While moms may live worlds apart, both figuratively and literally, they still find common threads that offer them empathy throughout their daily routines.

CHRISTINE LOUISE HOHLBAUM

My second book, *SAHM I Am*, came out in German so it felt like having Irish twins (15 months apart!) Once it has been successfully launched in the German market, I look forward to pursuing other non-fiction projects I have. The good news is I know what I am getting into now, so I can more carefully plan future projects to fit in with my current workload.

Being a published author establishes your credibility as someone with something important to say. I have done loads of PR consulting, speaking and other writing. I even sold a few pieces to national magazines. My main passion is in helping others succeed. When I see that smile of recognition in someone's eyes who has rediscovered his or her own greatness, I am paid back a thousand-fold.

Readers tell me I have empowered them to be more humorous in their own lives. The best feedback I could ever receive is someone saying, "You made a difference in my life today. Thank you." Much like a parent, we authors hear that too little, so it is enormously invigorating when someone takes the time to say it.

My daughter is a writer. At age seven, she puts together books, writes stories, and enjoys reading a great deal. My son is also interested in books and writing. The apple doesn't fall far from the tree.

As for my life path, the books I have written have forever changed me. A few stretchmarks here or there, a few more worry lines and a lot more laugh lines have marked my body, outlining the path I have chosen.

MARNA KRAJESKI

I'm planning to edit an anthology of stories written by other women called *Household Baggage Handlers*. I also have a manuscript in progress about family life while my husband was deployed. It's called *Unaccompanied Baggage*. I've been invited to speak at three spouse club meetings in California, Pennsylvania, and Massachusetts. That was a real honor.

CAROLINE POSER

I haven't slept in nearly six years (oldest son going on six). It has nothing to do with the book and everything to do with my children! Maybe I am insane...I am planning to do it all over again. I have another book I am working on that I want to publish next Spring. I feel compelled.

NINA MARIE DURAN

Next for me is teaching and mentoring. One of my passions is kids—which means anyone younger than me. One thing I really wanted to do was mentor teenagers, especially teenage moms. For me, mentoring them, talking to them, and having them get my books—that makes my day. To be a ray of light in their lives. There are 15 year-olds who read my book and 20 year-olds who say, "Oh girl!"

My book is not about how I delivered a baby, but about how a baby delivered me. When I go and give these girls my "testimony" it's about how Elijah makes me want to be a better person. Because of Elijah I am motivated. I refuse to sit back and accept less. Even if my presentation is just 40 minutes, at the end I know that I have planted a seed. If I can let just one young mom know that she's not alone, and she's normal, that's enough.

I love the path I am on. I read once, "What if finding the love of your life meant changing the life that you love?" That's a prime example of me—how I had a life with no responsibilities and then boom, I was pregnant, making huge decisions. I hope to help women understand to embrace their decisions, and not just learn from their mistakes, but learn to love your mistakes. Our mistakes can be blessings in disguise.

ARLENE SCHUSTEFF

I am happy to announce that I am going to be releasing an anthology called *Special Gifts: Women Writers on the Heartache, the Happiness and the Hope of Raising a Special Needs Child*. If you are the mother of a child with an emotional, behavioral or developmental disorder such as ADD, Asperger's Syndrome, Autism, Bi-Polar Disorder, Non-Verbal Learning Disability or PDD, this book is for you.

Special Gifts is filled with heartfelt, emotional essays from mothers dealing with their child (or a relative) with special needs. I asked questions such as: When did you suspect that your child was different from other children? Was there one defining moment or a general feeling? How did the news impact you? Your spouse? Your other children? Your parents? How is your child unique? Have you learned to see beyond the label, how? How does your child relate to others? What are her greatest difficulties? What are his greatest strengths? What has he taught you that you might not have learned? How has having a child with special needs impacted your relationships with your friends? Are you nervous about the future? What does the future hold? Is your child aware of her differences? How do you explain them to him and others? What are you scared of? What are you happy about? What are you angry about?

Special Gifts is NOT an advice book, but rather essays on the emotional journey.

PAMELA JO LEO

I don't have to die without ever accomplishing my life's dream. My friend Larry Cohen, who wrote *Playful Parenting*, told me the best part of publishing his book was all the people he met, and I have to echo that sentiment. I cannot tell you what it feels like to get calls from all over the world. A woman from Kentucky just called me and said, "I want five books, I'm going to Hong Kong and there's a woman there who wants one." I asked her, "How does someone in Hong Kong know about my book?" She said she had heard me on the radio.

I've learned that people who hear the message, and want to live in a world where children are raised with connection, are willing to be seed planters all over the world.

TERILEE HARRISON

While people got excited about the book, they were even more excited about my radio show for moms. I had an ah-ha! moment. I was doing every women's event I could. In November I was in Atlantic City, looking at the other ocean across the country, on the phone with my son in Southern California. He turned five that week, and he was sobbing, "I miss you so much, when are you coming home?" I was looking out the window from my beautiful suite in the Taj Mahal Hotel, and my limo was right there, and it was all so glamorous. And I realized it wasn't time in my career for such big speaking engagements. When he's ten, he probably won't be sobbing so much.

So I've had an opportunity to build a radio show, from home, and have met such wonderful people. There are lots of opportunities today to be involved in internet radio. I don't want anyone to think that it is difficult to do. There are many different venues to choose from—if you're reaching moms, MomsRadioNetwork.com has a lot of mom shows grouped together. I am with BigMediaUSA.com, but there's also World Talk Radio and Hay House Radio. When I first went out and met the people at BigMedia I'd never met anyone who was so excited to meet me. They knew that the moms who were previously at World Talk Radio were at 70,000 listeners. They knew that moms are hot. Whatever your niche is, there is a venue for you. It's all on the Internet, it's all archived. People can listen on their own schedule. It's a great way to build your platform and meet people because everyone will want to be a guest on your show.

Here is the intro to my show: "The Business Mom Connection—the talk show for moms in business who are doing it all and juggling it all! Each week you will be enlightened, encouraged, and informed as you are connected with everything important to you as a mom business owner. Show host Terilee Harrison, The Business Mom, will introduce you to successful business moms and bring you the latest resources and not-to-be-missed events for moms in business. Terilee will connect you with expert mentors in the business areas that matter to you most—communications, marketing, negotiation, networking, public relations, publishing, and sponsorship (to name a few.) This show is more than merely learning how to grow a thriving business! Terilee and her guests and expert mentors will also share their personal stories and tips for bringing you more life and less overwhelm, how to maintain sanity and survive as an entrepreneurial couple, or how to achieve strength and serenity as a single mom in business." Isn't it great?

I am working on my next book *Sanity and Survival Strategies for Entrepreneurial Couples*. And I am excited about following that up with *Strength and Serenity Secrets for Single Moms in Business*. I feel if anyone needs the extra support its the moms doing it by themselves.

KATHRYN MAHONEY

Am I planning on more books or other products? I think so. I just don't know what or when. I have some thoughts rattling around in my brain. Only time will tell when I'm ready to let the rest of the world in on them.

I got a gig writing an article for a magazine as a result of writing my book and being affiliated with my publisher. It was great and I hope more things will come. I also own a home-based marketing communications company, which helps pay the bills. I think adding "published author" to my list of credentials helps secure some work.

I never dreamed of being a humor writer, it just sort of "happened." And I really believe it happened for a reason. I feel like this is the path that God wants me to travel. Works for me. I love it!

I hope that my children will realize how important having a sense of humor really is—life can be so difficult sometimes, and if you can laugh about the stupid stuff instead of taking it so seriously, it will be a much better journey!

I can't think of a better gift than to make people laugh. So if I can do that by writing about my crazy family, than I feel very blessed!

CHRISTIE GLASCOE CROWDER

Writing *Your Big Sister's Guide* opened me to more sisterly advice that I would love to share with all of the little sisters of the world. I have toyed around with a guide for planning a wedding, and a guide to your first pregnancy. It also made me reflect on the relationship I had with my parents, particularly my father. I would like to write a book on Dads and Daughters.

I am still a *free*-lancer of sorts. I am hoping that once my book is out there and I make more appearances, some income will be seen. I never embarked on this journey to be a bestselling author. This was truly a labor of love for my sister and girlfriends as well as a test for me. When I am faced with challenging things, sometimes I get scared halfway through and want to give up. This was something I wanted and needed to see through and I am so glad I did.

LEEDA BACON

I remember saying to my husband Stan after the 40 hour labor and difficult birth of our son Ian, that I would never do that again. But three years later, our beautiful daughter, Amy was born. It is so miraculously incredible that you can forget about all the pain you experienced during childbirth and think about having another one. Writing a second book after all the sweat and hard work put into your first seems impossible, but then ideas start popping into your head. Personally, I have at least two more books that are tumbling around in my brain; one on art and how it relates to dieting and another on positive aging. I also look forward to nurturing my first book through speaking engagements and being active in creating a line of products. The sky is the limit when you truly believe in something.

MALONDA RICHARD

I have decided to do a traveling exhibition that will include various multimedia elements instead of a traditional book tour. In preparation for this project, I spent months searching for inspiration in the arts and eventually came up with the concept of creating multimedia products (posters, video , etc.) as a way to bring my readers into the world of my book.

I am planning to tie in several products with my book and I am definitely going to write more books in the future.

I hope that the book will inspire my daughter, and my future children, to achieve all of their wildest dreams.

I pray that readers will be inspired to love themselves and others in a much more profound way. The great thing about accomplishing a goal is that once people know that you did, they convince themselves that they can do it too.

SAMANTHA GIANULIS

This whole motherhood thing can swallow someone if they're not careful. I'm not being ungrateful, I'm not giving a disclaimer about motherhood, I am giving my opinion—you have to learn balance as a woman, (wife) and mother, or your enjoyment and enthusiasm for life stands to be substantially decreased. I've seen it happen. I felt it happening to me.

When I wasn't a published writer, I dreamed about being one some-day. I made my goal known to my family. But sometimes life just gets in the way of everything, and my dreams were put on hold while I put out some fires and scattered the ashes. When the dust settled, I had a lot to write about.

Now that I have this chance, I am holding on tooth and nail. Because I know it is a chance to develop something within me, for me, and ultimately, for others—starting with the little people who stand by my computer, tapping me on the shoulder, "Momma, are you done writing? I'm hungry."

No one ever achieved anything sacrificing themselves or their dreams. Rather, it creates resentment, unease, subconscious acts of bitterness. Those things are unworthy motivators, leading to an unhappy ending.

Fires break out. Ideas go awry. Dreams have to be paused. It doesn't stop the creative process waiting to break free...it's all writing material.

It's all one big story...waiting to be published.

Our Favorite Resources and Tips for Mom Writers

CHRISTINE LOUISE HOHLBAUM

My favorite resources for writing, publishing, promoting, publicity, and platform-building:

- Joan Stewart's *Publicity Hound* newsletter is a great resource.

- Check out PR agencies websites such as WasabiPublicity.com to see how one-page story sheets are developed. Another great resource, run by the same firm, is their online press kit solution called www.presskit247.com.

- Whatever you do, get a website. Avoid free ones with flashy banner ads. Subscribe to my marketing ezine, *The Author's Companion PR Postcard* at www.authorscompanion.com and buy a copy of the CD-Rom *The Author's Companion*. It is a turn-key marketing system designed to build a powerful platform instantly.

Remember that book promotion is a marathon, not a sprint. Take your time, develop your mailing list, cultivate relationships, and above all, be sincere. Remember when pitching to the media that they understand you want exposure, but they primarily care about your message.

Just as a child throws a tantrum, and it's not about you; it's also not about the book. It is about what you bring to this world and the people you help in the process.

If I were to give you three bits of advice, they would be:

- Maintain focus. Set goals and don't let life's little distractions pull you away from what is truly important.

- Understand it is a roller coaster ride. You will experience a heightened sense of joy and moments of despair. It is normal.

- Remember you are an expert at something. You've written an entire book. Now go out there and get them. As my mama always says, "Just show up!"

My personal mantra is—when I hear "no", I also hear "next". Not everyone will be enthused by what you bring to the table. So what? Next!

JULIE WATSON SMITH

My favorite resources are fellow authors!

My top tips for you, the reader and soon-to-be-published writer:

- Write because you love it, not because you expect to make money.
- Write what you know and what you are passionate about.
- Read everything from trade books to trashy novels.
- A bonus tip — Expect to spend 85% on PR and 15% on everything else.

My biggest mistake, what I learned:
Shortly after the release of my book, I was hit by several challenges in my personal life. Rather than giving myself permission to handle life, I beat myself up over not working harder on the book. This caused me to feel even more deflated. It took several months to get my focus back and realize that I cannot control—or ignore—life's unexpected events. Now, I'm able to nurture myself, my family and my career.

Revisit and revise your marketing plan often to allow for changes in your life and the world.

My three personal mantras are:
- Live an inspired life with a pure heart.
- Always learn, live and love the chaos of mommyhood.
- Inspire your imagination.

IRIS WAICHLER

There are a number of great resources for writing and publishing out there. Expose yourself to as much as possible. I found the Mom Writer's Co-Op while reading a magazine article. Read as much as you can in magazines and newspapers that might address your topic of interest. You will find names and resources there to help you on your project. For both of my books I went to the bookstore and looked to see what was already out there. I noted the publishers and style of the books that were successful and this helped me decide who to approach and what new things I could do. *Writer's Guide* is an excellent resource to learn about specialty publishers. The Internet is an incredible, endless resource. I just put in my topic and began searching and found names, information, and places to go to gather information, ideas, and people who could help me move toward my publication goal.

One of the biggest and best surprises for me has been the amazing network of talented people associated with the co-op. There are many components to getting a book published and sold which I had no experience with, but were necessary pieces of the bookselling process. The other members of the co-op made this process so easy. I just put out an email asking if somebody knew the answer to a question and without fail they answered my pleas.

My biggest mistake was approaching some publishers before my book was in its final form. I was anxious to get my book project going and assumed they would offer some editing expertise but that resulted in some rejections. In retrospect I should have waited and been more patient before I approached them with my final product.

I wish I had known from the beginning how tight the publishing market had gotten since I wrote my previous book. That would have helped me temper my expectations into a more reasonable framework, and reduced my frustration level. I wish I'd had more experience with the marketing and Internet elements of doing a book. That also would have made this whole process easier for me.

For me with my skill set and experience, writing the book was a lot easier than marketing it. I also learned that it is tricky to take a topic that you believe has a relatively large target group and convince other people that you have something fresh and innovative to say about it. Packaging your goods is a critical challenge in the publishing world.

I was lucky that I picked a topic that I was personally and professionally passionate about. I knew in my heart and gut that I had something to say that was useful to people, and that it could make a real difference in how they emerged from this difficult journey. That kept me focused and writing the book and contacting publishers even after the rejection slips started coming. When publishers told me there was no market for the topic because not enough people cared about it, that made me even more determined to get the book out there. If you believe in what you are writing, don't let anybody or anything stop you from making it become a reality. I am proud that I assumed this stance and the responses I have received from people in this early phase have been incredibly rewarding.

I am hopeful that as my daughter gets older, she will also be proud of my efforts, since it is really her story.

∽◯

KATHRYN MAHONEY

My top 3 tips for you, the reader and soon-to-be-published writer:

- Plan early, and plan often. The more of a marketing plan you have before you even approach a publisher, the better. Your publisher wants to know how you're going to get the word out about the book and the more you have in place ahead of time, the easier it will be for you to promote the book once it's released.

- Enjoy the journey! The process of publishing a book can be daunting, but it's such a huge accomplishment and you should be proud of it. Take it for what it is…one of many rewarding life experiences. Don't get bogged down in the sales figures or your Amazon rankings. Pat yourself on the back for simply getting your book published. Not too many people can lay claim to that.

- Don't lose sight of what really matters in life…family and friends. Don't stick your kids in front of the television to watch a marathon of videos so you can write, or turn down invitations to be with friends because you can't peel yourself away from the computer. Writing and success can wait. You've only got one shot at being with your children and watching them grow and achieve their milestones. Don't miss out on that.

My biggest mistake:

Not having more of a marketing plan before I submitted my manuscript. It definitely takes several months to gather the contacts you want to approach when your book is complete. If you have all of this information ahead of time, it makes it much easier when you're ready to launch the book. I felt like I was researching and promoting at the same time, which wasn't nearly as effective.

I wish I had known, or expected:
How much it costs to successfully promote a book and how little you actually make per book when sold in stores.

My advice:
Really ask yourself *why* you want to write this book and what you hope to get out of the process. Stay true to that. Don't let others determine what the goal of your book should be. It's YOUR book!

LEEDA BACON

The best resource and inspiration for writing is life. Whatever you have experienced in life, good or bad, can help guide a reader who may be walking down the same path. You could be the one who makes their journey a safe passage. Sharing your hard-earned knowledge might encourage someone to keep going and lead them victoriously to the other side.

My 3 tips for the reader:
- Believe in yourself
- Believe in your product
- Believe that you can reach the stars.

My favorite encouragement or mantra: Be Ye Encouraged!

CHRISTIE GLASCOE CROWDER

My favorite writing resource is Microsoft OneNote. I absolutely love it. It is like having a tabbed spiral notebook on your computer screen. If you are obsessed with categorizing and sticky-noting, this program is for you. It takes the hassle out of creating several word files and folders but it does work with Word. Being that not everyone has OneNote, you can easily transfer your OneNote documents to Word Documents. This program made writing my book and keeping my notes organized a breeze. I highly recommend it.

My other favorite resource, though expensive, is the Tablet PC. This is a laptop computer that has a screen you can write on. Your handwriting converts to typed text. A writer's dream to not have to re-type handwritten notes. It's also a great tool for teachers or editors. If your students/clients email papers to you, you can write your comments on screen and email it back. As soon as you can afford one, I would get one.

Motherly Advice:
The biggest piece of advice I can give aspiring writers is don't doubt yourself. You ARE a writer! It starts from within and it grows with a support system. Surround yourself with people who love and believe in you. We know you have a voice and we want to hear it!

MARNA KRAJESKI

What I learned is promoting the book is every bit as much work as writing it. Sort of like having Irish twins—you have a baby and right away find out you're pregnant again. The work never stops.

My tips:
- Hire someone to write or rewrite fabulous news releases for you until you learn the ropes yourself.

- Spring for a professional headshot. Those photographs go out everywhere.

- It takes a long time to grow a baby and sometimes the growth is very subtle.

MALONDA RICHARD

My top 3 tips:

- Have faith that somebody out there will love your work.

- Never, ever give up your dream of becoming a published author.

- Build a support team of people to help you get your book sold to as many people as humanely possible.

My biggest mistake was not having a think-tank of readers to review my manuscript before I got my book publishing deal. I really wished I had taken time to get a committed group of friends together so I wouldn't have to worry about who was going to give me creative feedback.

I wish I had known more about the book industry and distribution. I wish I had known that writing and publishing a book is not an instant ticket to becoming rich.

My favorite quote is from Marian Wright Edelman, "You were born God's original. Try not to become someone's copy."

My personal mantra is: The work is hard but the rewards are great.

NINA MARIE DURAN

The one thing I wish is that I could have been a little more financially stable, or had a back-up plan. I didn't anticipate how financially challenging it is. If I had to give one piece of advice to would-be writers, it's to have a financial cushion.

My tips:

- Surround yourself with other people who believe in you and your book. That gave me the extra push on those days I felt like—this is hard, I can't do this.

- Find one other published author to piggyback on. I found Daniel San Miquel, author of *The Winter of My Years*. He's brilliant. He gave me completely unbiased opinions of my book along the way. He could tell me, "Yeah, this is great," or "No, you need to take this out." You need that one person who can tell you this is material that can be published. The last thing you want to do is give it to your husband, your boyfriend, your girlfriend.

ARLENE SCHUSTEFF

My attitude— if I put my mind to it, I can accomplish it (with everything except dieting). There was never the option that it wouldn't happen.

My favorite resources were media bistro, craigslist, Yahoo groups, *Writer's Digest*.

My tips for you:

- Believe in yourself.
- Enjoy the journey. It's not just about the end results.
- Don't take "no" for an answer.
- Be able to laugh, and positively react no matter what happens.

MAUREEN FOCHT

My advice:

- Have some money to work with; you really can't do this without money.
- Don't be afraid to get professional help. I hired a writer who had published before to help me write the book. You really need someone to mentor you, to help you through the whole process.
- Realize it is a complex, and a very competitive business. You definitely have to have a goal that's much bigger than making a buck on the book. It's about touching people.

PAMELA JO LEO

My tips:

- If you're going to hire a professional publicist make sure you have the time to work with them. Be very clear on what they will expect

- Once your book is out there it takes on a life of its own. Days when I was so mired in family stuff that I couldn't have taken a phone call for an interview, somebody else in who-knows-where was talking about it and someone else was ordering it on Amazon. Not that you should sit back and do nothing!

- Document everything—especially media attempts and successes.

It didn't take 20 years to write the book, but it took 20 years to line up my allies. It only took a few months to write. There was a ready and waiting market, with lots of people who knew my work for so many years.

All the support from the co-op and my publisher gave me the drive above and beyond my own intentions. I want to vindicate everyone's faith in the book. I want this book to sell like mad for many reasons, but one is to show that Wyatt-MacKenzie knows how to pick a good one.

To have people call me up and say I helped their family re-connect, is just incredible

NANCY C. CLEARY

My tips:

- Honestly assess the size of your platform. Dive into Part Two of this book with an open mind and peruse the publishing options proportional to your reach, or expand your platform and increase your options.

- Publishing a book is a business endeavor, and should be treated as such. The amount of money you spend will be reflected in the size of your brand—and it is up to you to parlay this brand equity for larger visibility and larger paying gigs, which in turn however may cost you in time away from the family.

- You control your reaction to everything that happens on your publishing journey. The positive energy—patience, understanding, compassion and grace—that you give to all the experts, vendors, customers, reviewers, and your publishers, will get you far!

DEBORAH HURLEY

Defining myself as a writer and understanding what writing means to me...

Some write to instruct while others write to inspire. Some write to encourage while others write to argue. One writer may write to reveal, and another to touch our emotions, and yet another to explain why. Some writers scoop us up and take us to faraway lands while others keep us focused on the here and now.

I spent a lot of time wondering what kind of writer I was and if I was actually a writer at all. I used to think that writers were people who had to be editors, reporters, English majors, or people with lots of prestigious degrees. I used to think that to be a writer you had to be in some type of elite group, win awards for your work or belong to all sorts of writers clubs. I used to believe that to write something and have it published, you had to know someone who could help you make it all happen, and I used to believe that authors were people who were "better" than me. Well, all of my "used to" thoughts have changed.

What I know is that I did not go to a prestigious college; instead I completed three years at a State University while suffering with depression and anxiety. What I know is that I never belonged to any writers groups; instead I spent a decade nurturing my babies and enduring my illness. I had never written an article for a magazine or newspaper and I never knew anyone in the business. What I most certainly know now is that no one person is "better" than me and I absolutely know that I have always loved to write and that my writing has always come from my heart.

What I know is that I do not write to instruct; I write to evoke emotion. I never had a group of people rallying around me, supporting me, encouraging me and telling me that I was capable of writing. What I did have was a belief in myself and that belief outweighed my doubts, my fears and the confusion that I had on where and how to begin. What I did have was the unstoppable desire to have my work published. I had a vision of holding my book, going to book signings and above all, embracing someone who had read my work and been touched by it. I pictured myself holding the hand of another woman who had been affected by severe depression. In my heart I knew that my words could make a difference. The belief I had in myself is what I clung to and ultimately what carried me and pushed me forward to getting published.

In closing...proof of how Deborah Hurley's book has touched her readers, here are a few of her unsolicited Amazon reviews:

A book to encourage others, May 11, 2007

I recently read this book on vacation. This book is a must read. Even if you have never suffered from depression, this book gives you an inside look at what it's like to suffer from this disease. I'm amazed at the struggles Debbie has endured over the years. She gives hope to all the people out there suffering from this horrible disease. This book will certainly change the life of anyone who reads it. If you don't understand what depression is, after you read this, you will have a new understanding of the severity of it. You will no longer just tell people who suffer from depression to "snap out of it" as you will have a full understanding of the mind of someone who suffers from it. Deborah, this was a wonderful book and I'm sure you will make a difference in many peoples lives.

Very Touching!, March 22, 2007

I read this book in just 1 day on my way into NYC/work on the train. I couldn't put it down... my thoughts, actions and emotions were on fire throughout the entire read of the book. You truly never realize what life throws at each individual person... You are an amazing person to put your words on paper for the world to see in hopes of helping someone else. Congratulations on your new life.

A look inside depression, March 8, 2007

A fabulous insight to one woman's life...*Fragments of Hope* takes you through the life of a true survivor of clinical depression. Deborah shows her journey through her thoughts, feelings, trials and triumphs! This is a MUST read for anyone yearning to understand the whys of this illness and at the same time gives hope to those suffering that help is out there and you CAN make it through. I especially enjoyed the poetry written throughout the book. What makes this book stand out is that it is not a medical history, but a personal one.

Great Job! February 18, 2007

Deborah Hurley does an outstanding job of providing insight into depression. It is a powerful book that has you praying for her recovery from this paralyzing illness. Deborah is a courageous person whose first hand account sheds light on a greatly misunderstood illness.

A Courageous Journey, February 3, 2007

Deborah Hurley does an outstanding job describing her emotional struggle with serious depression. I read this book in its entirety, in one sitting. I was immediately drawn into this author's mind and heart. I wanted to reach out and take her hand in mine. I came away with a new understanding of the depths of this debilitating disease.

Deborah writes with a rare combination of courage and hope. This book is not just essential reading for anyone who has experienced depression in some form but also for people who have suffered some sort of pain and heartache in their life. This book's message, that hope is within our reach is powerful. Congratulations Deborah!

Bravo!, January 25, 2007
Thank you Deborah for writing this book. In my own life, I never suffered from depression however, I do have a family member that does and had no idea what it was like until I read your book. I was very blind to what the disease does to someone and my heart was breaking for you when I read the book! I am so glad that you were able to fight and come back to write this book. Thank you again for helping me understand depression and I am going to pass my book onto my sister to help her.

Wow! , January 18, 2007
What an emotional journey this author takes you on. Deborah Hurley shares her life and exposes herself in so many ways. I read this book in one sitting. I could not put it down. Fantastic!

PART TWO

*"I write so that my handful of pebbles,
tossed each day into still waters,
can create a ripple."*

~ ANNE SCHROEDER
author of *Ordinary Aphrodite*

CHAPTER 8

The Secret & Science

to Getting Your Book Published

*W*OULD IT SURPRISE YOU TO KNOW ANYONE can get published? If you know the options, and understand the principles of publishing, all you need to do is apply energy—and *a lot* of it.

You're not a writer? You can find professionals who can help. Professional writer? You will soon see how your experience and talent can put you in the path of a major publishing deal. Or if you simply have a passion, and a purpose for a book—here is how to manifest your ideas into book form.

I presented this information as an interactive online class throughout 2007. I invite you to experience it yourself in color with audio and video. (*For access email:* nancy@wymacpublishing.com with subject: SECRET CLASS.)

In Tech Talk I'll tell you ways you can share this empowering knowledge with others.

Whether you are a professional writer looking for a literary agent to land a New York publishing deal, or you are a funny mom wanting to put a book of her blog entries together... there is a publishing option for you.

IN THIS CHAPTER

The Alchemy of Publishing

Defining & Measuring the 4 Principles

The 4 Publishing Options

Tech Talk — What to do Next...

The Alchemy of Getting Published

I believe there's a science to getting your book published, and there are secrets to how this whole crazy book industry works. I'd like to present "author alchemy"—the chemistry behind manifesting *and* marketing books.

What is the secret to getting published? It's all about energy. If you know how to *move* this energy, anyone can get published. The science is in the principles that make the energy move. The more energy you apply to each principle, the closer you are to your book, and the more successful your book will be.

Sound easy? Yes. Is it easy? No. But you can do it – if your passion is strong enough; if you know where to focus your efforts; and if your expectations are in proper perspective.

Book Energy

Every thought you have about your book, every page you write, everyone you tell you are writing a book – this is all energy sent into the Universe, attracting the means to manifest your book. Focus that energy in the direction of the publishing principles which follow.

Substance is created when the energy of an atom attracts similarly charged energy atoms and molecules form. All matter is made up of molecules—books included. Not just the paper, ink, and glue, but the words, the idea, the success – it all takes energy to manifest.

Many people have a book in them just waiting to come out, but only a few are devoted enough to do what it takes to make that book a reality. If you are ready to take the journey grab a pen and refer to the Principle Chart on the following pages, or download it and print in color:

www.wymacpublishing.com/PrinciplesChart.pdf

Building a Book Atom

We're going to create your books on a molecular level. The chart on pages 190 and 191 will be the "molecular structure" of your book. We are building a "book atom" and making it magnetic—to attract all the help you need!

Start at the Core

We're going to start at the center—the nucleus, the core. This is the heart of your book. The 4 Principles surrounding it will be affected and powered by this core. In this core is your intention—why you want to publish this book. This HAS to be what you are passionate about. This is your purpose. Write your intention in the center of the chart.

The nucleus also provides the power behind the magnetic pull of your book molecule. Surrounding your center must be all of the positive energy you can muster. What you feel you will attract. No matter what happens on your publishing journey, if you are able to remain grateful, joyful, and retain hope and happiness—then your journey will be fulfilling and satisfying, and so will all the people you touch along the way. Readers will be grateful, producers will be gracious, and vendors will be lined up ready to fulfill your every wish.

Do not allow negative energies to enter your mind or your book molecule, as hard as that may be at times. You can control how you react to every situation. For the benefit of your book, handle each with grace and compassion, and what you will attract will surpass your wildest dreams.

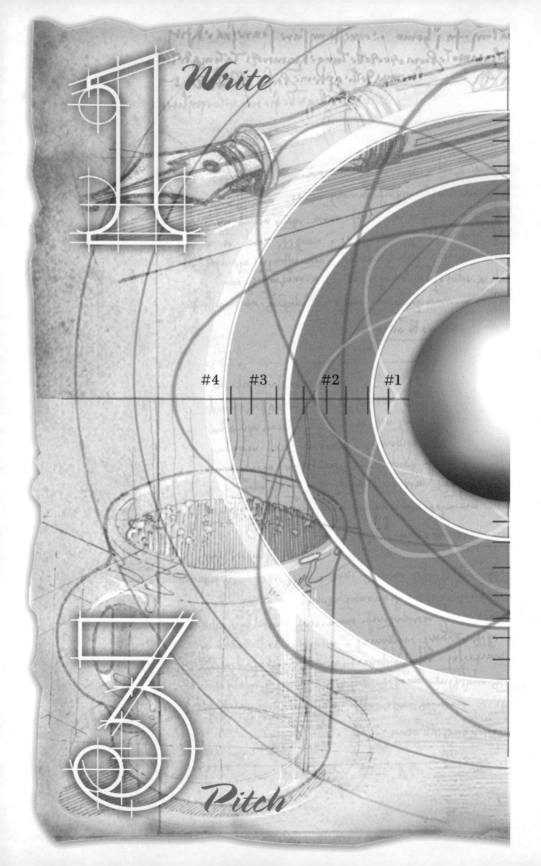

Defining & Measuring the 4 Principles

I believe the four principles of getting published are: Writing, Presence, Pitching, and finally, Publishing.

I will define each principle and you will measure how much energy you have applied to this point. If there are things you have not yet accomplished, you just need to apply more of your energy there!

Refer to the Principles Chart on page 190 and 191 to record your responses to the questions.

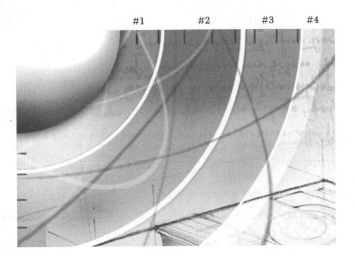

On the color chart Blue is #1 the closest to the nucleus, Red is #2, Orange is #3 and Yellow is #4 the furthest away.

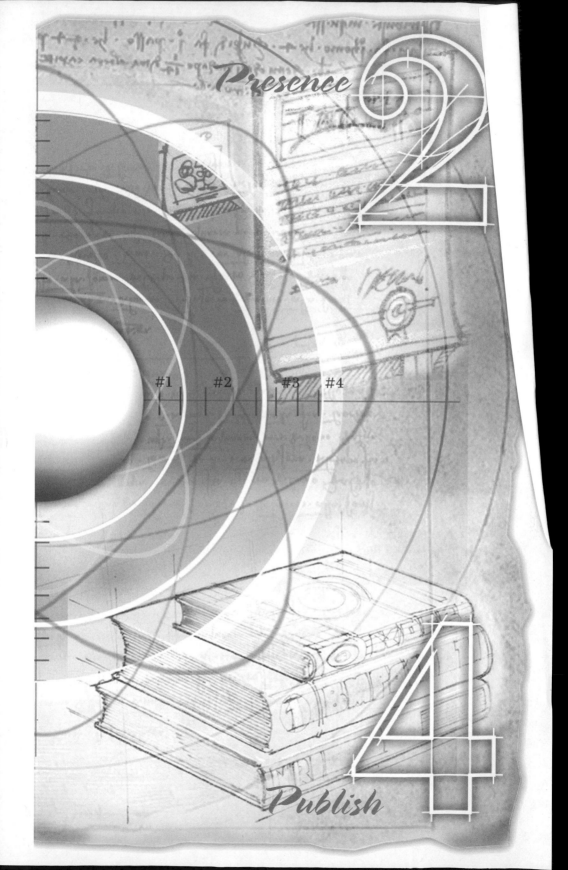

Writing Principle

If you want to publish a book, there's a good chance you are doing a lot of writing. I hope you are! This principle is "Write" but it is also includes "Read, Be Read, and Research."

Write – Write as much as possible. Get your words out there. Strive to improve—take classes, go to workshops, visit conferences. The Maui Writers Conference has always been my dream, but look closer—your local community college, or online classes from a variety of universities.

If you're *not* a writer, the option is hiring a ghostwriter. A number of the authors I have published worked with incredible ghostwriters to pull their ideas, workshops, or notes into publishable manuscript form. Refer to the Tech Tips from Chapter 1, (pages 12 14) on Ghostwriting, Editing, and Writing Coaching.

Be Read – Seek writing groups and peer reviewers, and develop your craft based on response from your market. You do not want to publish something that hasn't been read by individuals in your market and experts in your field. Find support groups –try eWPN, NAWW, Authors Guild, and search Yahoo writing groups. (*See Resource Section for info.*)

Research –Read as much as you can, especially books in your market and on your topic. It's time to go back to the core and revisit your purpose and why you want to publish. Are you staying on top of current events in your subject? Are you researching what's been written in the past about your topic? Do you know who the movers and shakers are in your market? Subscribe to *Writer's Digest*, and if you are really serious about researching other books before they hit the market subscribe to *Publisher's Weekly*. You can see who is getting book deals in your genre at *Publisher's Marketplace* (www.publishersmarketplace.com).

Measure Writing Principle

How much energy have you put into the Writing Principle? As you read each question, put a mark on the Principles Chart in the **top left** quadrant, in the appropriate ring, #1 is the closest to the center, and radiating outward are #2, #3, and #4 is the furthest out.

Answer about your writing experience:

1. If you have been writing for school, for your church's newsletter, or your company's newsletter, put a mark in #1.

2. If you are writing on your own blog daily, put a mark in #2.

3. If you have articles online – on your own website, syndicated on numerous other websites, and in newsletters, put a mark in #2.

4. If you are writing your own newsletter on the topic of your book and sending it out on a regular basis to a growing list of subscribers, put a mark in #2.

5. If you have created your own eBook so others can read and review your work, put a mark in #3.

6. If you have been published in an anthology, put a mark in #3.

7. If you have been writing for your local newspaper, put a mark in #3.

8. If you have a syndicated newspaper column, put a mark in #4.

9. If your writing is featured in national magazines, or you have your own magazine column, put a mark in #4.

Answer about the book you want to publish:

1. What format is your book idea currently in? If it is in your journals, put a mark in #1. If you have your table of contents done and your chapters organized, put a mark in #2. If it has been professionally edited, put a mark in #3.

2. If no one has read your manuscript, put a mark in #1. If you have had six or more people read your manuscript, put a mark in #2. if you

have had a dozen or more peers *and* experts read and provide critical feedback to your manuscript put a mark in #3.

Where have you developed your writing craft:

1. If you've completed high school and some college writing classes, put a mark in #1.

2. If you majored in journalism in college, or completed writing courses, put a mark in #2.

3. If you've attended writing conferences, put a mark in #3.

4. If you teach classes in your expertise, or in any writing field, put a mark in #3.

5. If you are a professional writer with years of experience, put a mark in #4.

6. If you plan on hiring a professional ghostwriter, put a mark in #4.

How much have you researched and participated in your niche:

1. If you are reading the latest books published in your market and posting your personal reviews on Amazon, put a mark in #2.

2. If you follow the leading authors' blogs in your market and comment on them, or participate in forums on your topic, put a mark in #2

3. If you have a blog where you frequently review current books and comment on authors in the media, put a mark in #2.

4. If you are being asked by authors in your market to review and endorse their books, put a mark in #3.

5. If you were hired to write a blog for a high-profile website, newspaper or magazine, put a mark in #3.

Writing Principle Resources

· *Writer Mama* by Christina Katz is a fantastic resource for developing
  your writing, finding time to write as a busy mom, and building a
  power writing portfolio.

· Stay on top of research with Google Alerts and Yahoo Alerts – get feeds
  for keywords, competitive books, and experts on your topic.

*You should complete your own chart so you will be able to quantify the answers and
choose the best publishing option, but if you'd like a visual shortcut, each principle will
end with notes, like this:*

Write. Read. Research.

Write well. Write often. Get your words out there. Strive to improve.
Take classes, seek writing peers and reviewers, develop your craft.

Read as much as you can. Research your market thoroughly.
Go back to the core, your purpose and why you want to
publish this book – are you reading other books about
the topic, are you researching, staying on top of
current events?

peer reviews

Copy-Editing

Chapters

Table of Contents

Journal

Published in Anthology

Your Own Newsletter

Own Blog

Comment on Blogs

Ghostwriter

Contribute to Newsletter

Magazine Column

Read Books, Post Amazon Reviews

Posted Articles Online

Church Newsletter

Syndicated Newspaper Column

Contribute to Local Newspaper Column

Writing Conferences

High School

on Mailing List   # of hits on Blog   # of writing classes taken

In the Writing Principle the only shortcut is to hire a professional ghostwriter.

Presence Principle

Who are you? Who knows you? What do they know about you? Where has your writing appeared? Where have you appeared?

There are 4 Parts of Presence:

1. **Author Branding** – Returning to your core, this is how you visually, verbally, and emotionally represent YOU—your personality and your purpose. *Refer to Tech Talk pages 29-35 to see examples.*

2. **Platform** – This is what you stand for, and how many people care about it. Wherever you are an expert, you'll want to immerse yourself in that market. Everywhere people who are interested in your book's topic will be, that's where you want to be—in their favorite magazines, on their favorite websites, on the television shows they watch. You want to be the go-to person in that industry for your expertise. How do you get there? With:

3. **Media Presence** – This is your media-savvy combined with the ability to pitch yourself (Principle #3). If you are great in the initial 30-second interview, chances are you'll be a good guest. Start with radio and then do local TV. Perform well locally and use your success to show national TV you've got what it takes.

4. **Bigger Presence** – Know there is a force responding to your energy, moving it toward manifestation. You must believe the Universe is on your side and wants to help you create your book.

Measure Presence Principle

How much energy have you put into the Presence Principle? As you read each question, put a mark on the Chart in the **top right** quadrant.

Author Branding:

1. If you have business cards that beautifully and succinctly represent you and your brand (with your photo, logo, colors, slogan) that yo u send with every correspondence and leave behind at every event, put a mark in #2.

2. If you have bookmarks and postcards with a quiz on your topic, or some helpful tips, whatever would appeal to your audience, put a mark in #2.

3. If you have a website which clearly expresses your specialty and has valuable offerings to your market, put a mark in #2.

4. If you have a blog with a banner which represents you with images and words, put a mark in #2.

5. If you have t-shirts, coffee mugs and hats you can offer as giveaways that spread your message, put a mark in #2.

Size of your Platform:

1. If you have 2-10 people visiting your blog or website a day, put a mark in #1. If there are 10-100 people visiting a day, put a mark in #2. If there are 100-500 people reading a day put a mark in #3, and if over 500 hitting your blog and/or site, put a mark in #4.

2. Where have you been seen discussing your topic? If it's in your local community doing events, or speaking at schools, libraries, churches, city council, or support groups put a mark in #1. If you've been on the local news, put a mark in #2. If people have read about you, or read your writing in the local newspaper, put a mark in #2. If they have read about you in their favorite magazines, put a mark in #3. If they-have seen you on national TV, put a mark in #4.

3. If you have been asked to be a spokesperson in your local community for the chamber of commerce, or at event at the library, or speak at a

fundraiser affecting your market, put a mark in #2. If you've been paid to be a speaker at an event, put a mark in #3. If you've been called by reporters to comment on current situations or trends in your market, or by producers to be a guest on TV, put a mark in #4.

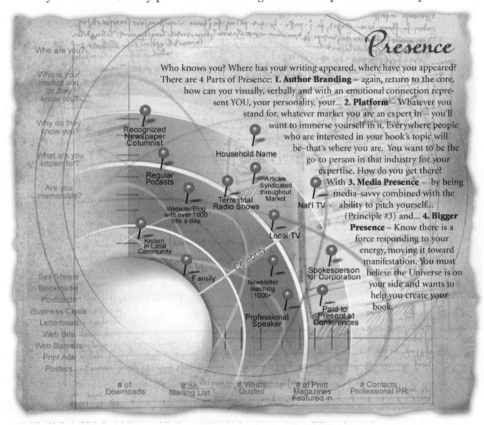

The only shortcut in the Presence Principle is being a celebrity or having a close friend who is one!

Presence Principle Resources

· GetKnownNow.com can help you fine-tune your presence.

· PressKit247.com puts your most important information in one place for media to find you. Its easy interface lets *you* post clippings, footage, and media successes as they happen, without paying your webmaster.

Pitch Principle

If you want a major book deal you will most likely need to go through an agent. To land an agent you must send them a pitch for your book proposal. And, the book proposal itself is one big pitch–combined with your presence and ability to write and research. Then, when you have books in hand you must be constantly selling–not just the book, but YOU–your unique and passionate contribution to this market.

How to pitch, who to pitch, when to pitch and what to pitch...every aspect of the publishing process involves pitching yourself, your book idea, your expertise, and most importantly, your ability to attract an audience.

How do you rank highly in the Presence Principle? You pitch something of value. You find the hook which will connect you with their audience.

Success comes when preparation meets opportunity. A pitch either *creates* the opportunity, or *responds to* an opportunity. Research keeps you abreast of opportunities in your market; your pitch opens the door; and your platform and author branding back you up.

The better your pitch, the more you have to offer and the more you know your audience. A successful pitch leads to more visibility, and more visibility attracts the individuals needed to manifest your book's success.

Measure Pitch Principle

How much energy have you put into the Pitch Principle? As you read each question, put a mark on the Chart in the **bottom left** quadrant.

Answer about pitching experience:
1. If you pitched an event, meeting, or party that resulted in a big turnout, put a mark in #1.
2. If you have sold tickets to an event, or raffled off something you created, or offered to raise money for charity, put a mark in #2.
3. If you placed press releases on wire services, or articles on syndication websites, and attracted readers, hits, and downloads, put a mark in #2.
4. If you pitched an op-ed piece to a newspaper and it got published, put a mark in #2.
5. If you have offered your services to speak at a conference and your proposal was accepted, put a mark in #2.
6. If you have sent your writing to magazines and it has been published, put a mark in #3.
7. If you have pitched your book proposal to a literary agent or editor at a publishing house (whether they responded or not), put a mark in #3.

Answer about PR:
1. If you have worked with a PR company or publicity agent in the past in any capacity, put a mark in #2.
2. If you hired a professional PR consultant to help build your platform, put a mark in #3.
3. If you hired a professional PR agent to work with you on media training and to pitch you to appropriate venues over a 3-6 month contract, put a mark in #3 on the very outside close to the next level.

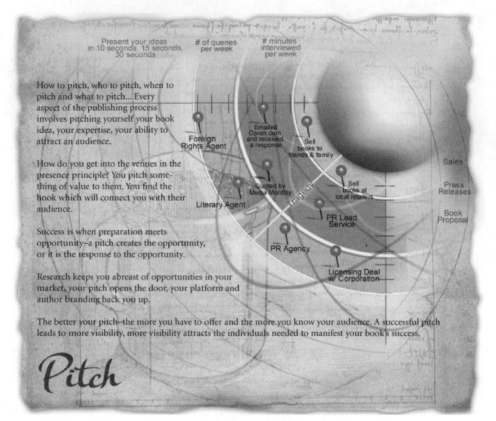

Sadly, the one shortcut to pitching is through tragedy, which brings the media *to* you, clamoring for your attention and story. Obviously, no one wants to undergo a tragedy just to write and pro mote a book, but using a tragedy to write a book that pays tribute or shows a way to help others heal from trauma or catastrophe, can be a powerful media magnet.

Pitch Principle Resources

- AuthorsCompanion.com has products and PR consulting services to help you hone your pitch and provides strategies for pitching proactively and reactively.
- ProfNet.com, or the simpler repackaged offering PRLeads.com, both send you media opportunities, it's up to you to respond providing exactly what the reporter or producer may need.

Publish Principle

In looking at the four levels, you have probably noticed that the further out from the center you go, the further along you are on the publishing path. Your writing ability is more developed, your platform larger, your pitches more succinct and relevant, and your media savvy greater. Now you are ready to look at your options for publishing.

Measure Publish Principle

How much energy have you put (or are you prepared to put) into the Publish Principle? Put a mark on the Chart in the **bottom right** quadrant.

PR investment:
1. How much money are you prepared to invest in PR? If it's under $1000, put a mark in #1. If it's between $1000-$2500, put a mark in #2. If between $2500-$5000, put a mark in #3, and if between $5000-$15,000 put a mark in #4.

2. What is your dream Advance—the money a major publisher will pay you upfront for your book idea, to be deducted from future sales? If you expect an advance or $1000-$2000, put a mark in #3; if it is $5000 -$50,000+, put a mark in #4.

Notice if the amount of money you are prepared to invest in PR matches the amount of money you expect for an advance—because that's exactly what publishers want you to spend it on—PR!

Expected Sales:
1. How many books do you expect to sell in the first year? If it's under 100 put a mark in #1; if it's between 100-1000 put a mark in #2; it it's between 1000 and 25,000 put a mark in #3; and if it's from 25,000 up to J.K. Rowling, put a mark in #4.

Evaluate your Chart

When you take a measured look at the 4 principles so far, then you are ready to apply the fourth principle. Take a good look at your marks. Are they concentrated more in one section than another?

Imagine a string connecting each mark, circling the center, spinning around like electrons around a nucleus. How far does your "author atom" expand? Now it is time to revisit the core . Ask yourself again, what is my intention in publishing this book? If you are passionate about your topic, an avid writer, and risk-taker, chances are what you have in front of you will be a glowing mass of efforts circling way out to the third and fourth levels.

Now quantify yourself in each of the principles. Then, based on your reach, choose your publishing option. The following pages describe the options for each level. You can choose your option to match your current markings, *or* you can focus more energy on each principle, and see how the laws of the Universe react as your book molecule expands.

The Science

Imagine this bundle of energy made of all your efforts becoming magnetized and attracting the connections and resources you need. Remember the positivity surrounding your core? You will be met with the same positive energy as you put out.

Now imagine how something you've written, or something you have left behind (a business card or bookmark), or a pitch you have made—which, while seemingly unsuccessful at the time, could get caught in the trajectory of your spiraling energy and make a connection somewhere else in the future. Imagine all of your efforts connecting, each one networking you to another great lead, sale or appearance. This is the chemistry—the actual transformation of the base idea to gold, and your book to profit. When your efforts reach critical mass and you create a nuclear chain reaction you create a Bestseller!

4 Publishing Options

Level #1 — Blue

Perhaps your publishing dreams aren't as grandiose as some of the other levels. Maybe you just want to give books to friends and family, and not spend any money on PR.

An **Author Service company** charges fees for each piece of the process from editing to basic book design and marketing services. They assign their ISBN, their name is on your book, they take a percentage of profit from retail, and mark up the books they sell to you (which is where they make a lot of profit.) Some well-known author service companies include: AuthorHouse, Aventine Press, Black Forest Press, Booklocker.com, BookPublisher, Cold Tree Press, Dog Ear Publishing, First Books, Infinity Publishing, iUniverse, Llumina Press, LuLu, Morgan James Publishing, Outskirts Press, PageFree Publishing, Publish America, SelfPublishing.com, Tabby House, Trafford Publishing, Universal Publishers, Unlimited Publishing, Virtualbookworm.com, WinePress Publishing, and Xlibris.

Though I don't endorse them, these companies are fine, and their services are fine. The drawbacks are 1) they take a percentage of your sales and mark up the cost of books; 2) they use a middleman you could use yourself; and 3) their name on your book leaves the stigma that you paid that company for an ISBN number and print-on-demand distribution.

Level #2 Red

A small independent press is the option for this level. If you know what a platform is, but haven't grown a huge one yet, this level is a great starting point for the first-time author. This, in essence, is YOU self-publishing.

The difference between publishing yourself and paying one of the author service companies in Level #1 is the owner of the ISBN. When it is your name on the spine (*the name you assign your own publishing entity which sounds like the perfect niche publisher for your book*), you collect 100% of the money directly and benefit from the brand you build.

When you self-publish you do not have to print a large press run of 1000-2000 books—in fact it is silly to do so before you have them sold! Using Ingram's Lightning Source print-on-demand company you can print as few or as many as you need. (This is the *same* printer the author service companies in Level #1 use.) Lightning will also distribute — meaning all of the retail sales for Amazon.com, BarnesandNoble.com, Target.com, Walmart.com and Ingram bookstore orders are filled automatically behind the scenes. You just collect the money!

Download the **Become Your Own Publisher Handbook** at www.wymacpublishing.com/BYOPabib.pdf for complete instructions. Here's a brief synopsis:

Step 1 - Name your publishing company and create an icon, and a brand you can be proud of.

Step 2 - Purchase an ISBN logbook at ISBN.org

Step 3 - Hire a publishing consultant, or use our BYOP Handbook to walk you through all of the publishing registrations.

Step 4 - Hire a book designer to create a powerful cover, back and spine and a professional interior layout. Use a professional who can get your files to perfect specifications.

Step 5 - Get an account with Lightning Source and have your designer upload files. Your book will appear on Amazon and all the other online retailers as well as available for special order through bookstores.

Become an Imprint!

Becoming an imprint of a larger publishing house is the ideal scenario for a new indie press to get launched. You will benefit from the brand that has already been built by the main "umbrella" publisher, yet you will

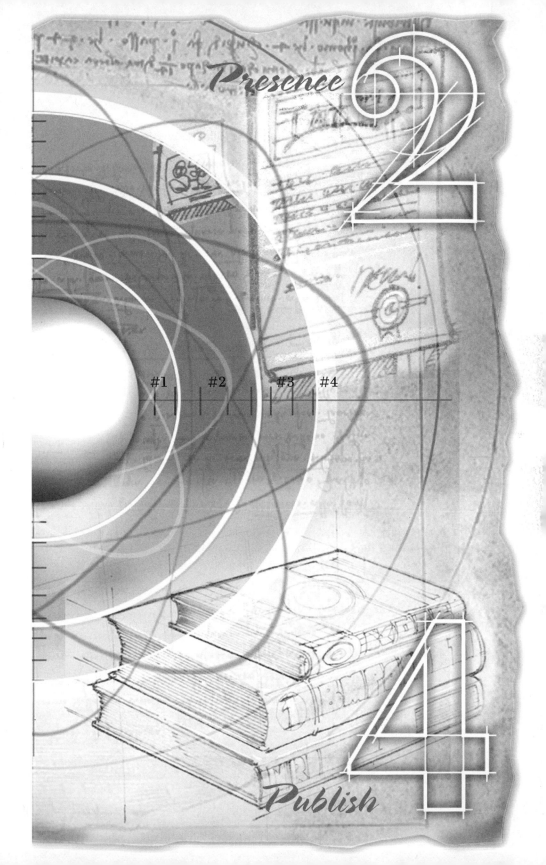

Presence

#1   #2   #3 #4

Publish

Defining & Measuring the 4 Principles

I believe the four principles of getting published are: Writing, Presence, Pitching, and finally, Publishing.

I will define each principle and you will measure how much energy you have applied to this point. If there are things you have not yet accomplished, you just need to apply more of your energy there!

Refer to the Principles Chart on page 190 and 191 to record your responses to the questions.

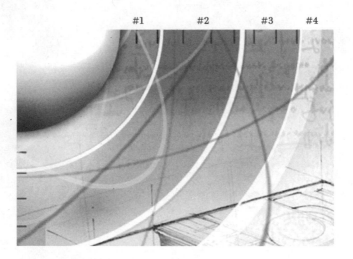

On the color chart Blue is #1 the closest to the nucleus, Red is #2, Orange is #3 and Yellow is #4 the furthest away.

Writing Principle

If you want to publish a book, there's a good chance you are doing a lot of writing. I hope you are! This principle is "Write" but it is also includes "Read, Be Read, and Research."

Write — Write as much as possible. Get your words out there. Strive to improve—take classes, go to workshops, visit conferences. The Maui Writers Conference has always been my dream, but look closer—your local community college, or online classes from a variety of universities.

If you're *not* a writer, the option is hiring a ghostwriter. A number of the authors I have published worked with incredible ghostwriters to pull their ideas, workshops, or notes into publishable manuscript form. Refer to the Tech Tips from Chapter 1, (pages 12-14) on Ghostwriting, Editing, and Writing Coaching.

Be Read — Seek writing groups and peer reviewers, and develop your craft based on response from your market. You do not want to publish something that hasn't been read by individuals in your market and experts in your field. Find support groups —try eWPN, NAWW, Authors Guild, and search Yahoo writing groups. (*See Resource Section for info.*)

Research —Read as much as you can, especially books in your market and on your topic. It's time to go back to the core and revisit your purpose and why you want to publish. Are you staying on top of current events in your subject? Are you researching what's been written in the past about your topic? Do you know who the movers and shakers are in your market? Subscribe to *Writer's Digest*, and if you are really serious about researching other books before they hit the market subscribe to *Publisher's Weekly*. You can see who is getting book deals in your genre at *Publisher's Marketplace* (www.publishersmarketplace.com).

Measure Writing Principle

How much energy have you put into the Writing Principle? As you read each question, put a mark on the Principles Chart in the **top left** quadrant, in the appropriate ring, #1 is the closest to the center, and radiating outward are #2, #3, and #4 is the furthest out.

Answer about your writing experience:

1. If you have been writing for school, for your church's newsletter, or your company's newsletter, put a mark in #1.

2. If you are writing on your own blog daily, put a mark in #2.

3. If you have articles online – on your own website, syndicated on numerous other websites, and in newsletters, put a mark in #2.

4. If you are writing your own newsletter on the topic of your book and sending it out on a regular basis to a growing list of subscribers, put a mark in #2.

5. If you have created your own eBook so others can read and review your work, put a mark in #3.

6. If you have been published in an anthology, put a mark in #3.

7. If you have been writing for your local newspaper, put a mark in #3.

8. If you have a syndicated newspaper column, put a mark in #4.

9. If your writing is featured in national magazines, or you have your own magazine column, put a mark in #4.

Answer about the book you want to publish:

1. What format is your book idea currently in? If it is in your journals, put a mark in #1. If you have your table of contents done and your chapters organized, put a mark in #2. If it has been professionally edited, put a mark in #3.

2. If no one has read your manuscript, put a mark in #1. If you have had six or more people read your manuscript, put a mark in #2. if you

have had a dozen or more peers *and* experts read and provide critical feedback to your manuscript put a mark in #3.

Where have you developed your writing craft:

1. If you've completed high school and some college writing classes, put a mark in #1.

2. If you majored in journalism in college, or completed writing courses, put a mark in #2.

3. If you've attended writing conferences, put a mark in #3.

4. If you teach classes in your expertise, or in any writing field, put a mark in #3.

5. If you are a professional writer with years of experience, put a mark in #4.

6. If you plan on hiring a professional ghostwriter, put a mark in #4.

How much have you researched and participated in your niche:

1. If you are reading the latest books published in your market and posting your personal reviews on Amazon, put a mark in #2.

2. If you follow the leading authors' blogs in your market and comment on them, or participate in forums on your topic, put a mark in #2

3. If you have a blog where you frequently review current books and comment on authors in the media, put a mark in #2.

4. If you are being asked by authors in your market to review and endorse their books, put a mark in #3.

5. If you were hired to write a blog for a high-profile website, newspaper or magazine, put a mark in #3.

Writing Principle Resources

· *Writer Mama* by Christina Katz is a fantastic resource for developing your writing, finding time to write as a busy mom, and building a power writing portfolio.

· Stay on top of research with Google Alerts and Yahoo Alerts – get feeds for keywords, competitive books, and experts on your topic.

You should complete your own chart so you will be able to quantify the answers and choose the best publishing option, but if you'd like a visual shortcut, each principle will end with notes, like this:

Write. Read. Research.

Write well. Write often. Get your words out there. Strive to improve.
Take classes, seek writing peers and reviewers, develop your craft.

Read as much as you can. Research your market thoroughly.
Go back to the core, your purpose and why you want to
publish this book – are you reading other books about
the topic, are you researching, staying on top of
current events?

peer reviews

Copy-Editing

Chapters

Table of Contents

Journal

Published in Anthology

Your Own Newsletter

Own Blog

Comment on Blogs

Ghostwriter

Magazine Column

Contribute to Newsletter

Read Books, Post Amazon Reviews

Posted Articles Online

Church Newsletter

Syndicated Newspaper Column

Contribute to Local Newspaper Column

Writing Conferences

High School

on Mailing List

of hits on Blog

# of writing classes taken

In the Writing Principle the only shortcut is to hire a professional ghost-writer.

Presence Principle

Who are you? Who knows you? What do they know about you? Where has your writing appeared? Where have you appeared?

There are 4 Parts of Presence:

1. **Author Branding** – Returning to your core, this is how you visually, verbally, and emotionally represent YOU–your personality and your purpose. *Refer to Tech Talk pages 29-35 to see examples.*

2. **Platform** – This is what you stand for, and how many people care about it. Wherever you are an expert, you'll want to immerse yourself in that market. Everywhere people who are interested in your book's topic will be, that's where you want to be–in their favorite magazines, on their favorite websites, on the television shows they watch. You want to be the go-to person in that industry for your expertise. How do you get there? With:

3. **Media Presence** – This is your media-savvy combined with the ability to pitch yourself (Principle #3). If you are great in the initial 30-second interview, chances are you'll be a good guest. Start with radio and then do local TV. Perform well locally and use your success to show national TV you've got what it takes.

4. **Bigger Presence** – Know there is a force responding to your energy, moving it toward manifestation. You must believe the Universe is on your side and wants to help you create your book.

Measure Presence Principle

How much energy have you put into the Presence Principle? As you read each question, put a mark on the Chart in the **top right** quadrant.

Author Branding:

1. If you have business cards that beautifully and succinctly represent you and your brand (with your photo, logo, colors, slogan) that yo u send with every correspondence and leave behind at every event, put a mark in #2.

2. If you have bookmarks and postcards with a quiz on your topic, or some helpful tips, whatever would appeal to your audience, put a mark in #2.

3. If you have a website which clearly expresses your specialty and has valuable offerings to your market, put a mark in #2.

4. If you have a blog with a banner which represents you with images and words, put a mark in #2.

5. If you have t-shirts, coffee mugs and hats you can offer as giveaways that spread your message, put a mark in #2.

Size of your Platform:

1. If you have 2-10 people visiting your blog or website a day, put a mark in #1. If there are 10-100 people visiting a day, put a mark in #2. If there are 100-500 people reading a day put a mark in #3, and if over 500 hitting your blog and/or site, put a mark in #4.

2. Where have you been seen discussing your topic? If it's in your local community doing events, or speaking at schools, libraries, churches, city council, or support groups put a mark in #1. If you've been on the local news, put a mark in #2. If people have read about you, or read your writing in the local newspaper, put a mark in #2. If they have read about you in their favorite magazines, put a mark in #3. If they-have seen you on national TV, put a mark in #4.

3. If you have been asked to be a spokesperson in your local community for the chamber of commerce, or at event at the library, or speak at a

fundraiser affecting your market, put a mark in #2. If you've been paid to be a speaker at an event, put a mark in #3. If you've been called by reporters to comment on current situations or trends in your market, or by producers to be a guest on TV, put a mark in #4.

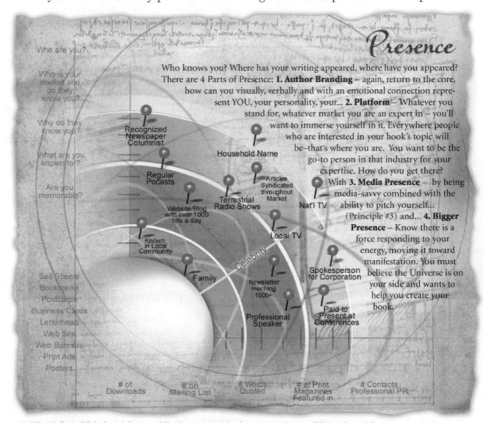

The only shortcut in the Presence Principle is being a celebrity or having a close friend who is one!

Presence Principle Resources

- GetKnownNow.com can help you fine-tune your presence.
- PressKit247.com puts your most important information in one place for media to find you. Its easy interface lets *you* post clippings, footage, and media successes as they happen, without paying your webmaster.

Pitch Principle

If you want a major book deal you will most likely need to go through an agent. To land an agent you must send them a pitch for your book proposal. And, the book proposal itself is one big pitch—combined with your presence and ability to write and research. Then, when you have books in hand you must be constantly selling—not just the book, but YOU—your unique and passionate contribution to this market.

How to pitch, who to pitch, when to pitch and what to pitch...every aspect of the publishing process involves pitching yourself, your book idea, your expertise, and most importantly, your ability to attract an audience.

How do you rank highly in the Presence Principle? You pitch something of value. You find the hook which will connect you with their audience.

Success comes when preparation meets opportunity. A pitch either *creates* the opportunity, or *responds to* an opportunity. Research keeps you abreast of opportunities in your market; your pitch opens the door; and your platform and author branding back you up.

The better your pitch, the more you have to offer and the more you know your audience. A successful pitch leads to more visibility, and more visibility attracts the individuals needed to manifest your book's success.

Measure Pitch Principle

How much energy have you put into the Pitch Principle? As you read each question, put a mark on the Chart in the **bottom left** quadrant.

Answer about pitching experience:

1. If you pitched an event, meeting, or party that resulted in a big turnout, put a mark in #1.

2. If you have sold tickets to an event, or raffled off something you created, or offered to raise money for charity, put a mark in #2.

3. If you placed press releases on wire services, or articles on syndication websites, and attracted readers, hits, and downloads, put a mark in #2.

4. If you pitched an op-ed piece to a newspaper and it got published, put a mark in #2.

5. If you have offered your services to speak at a conference and your proposal was accepted, put a mark in #2.

6. If you have sent your writing to magazines and it has been published, put a mark in #3.

7. If you have pitched your book proposal to a literary agent or editor at a publishing house (whether they responded or not), put a mark in #3.

Answer about PR:

1. If you have worked with a PR company or publicity agent in the past in any capacity, put a mark in #2.

2. If you hired a professional PR consultant to help build your platform, put a mark in #3.

3. If you hired a professional PR agent to work with you on media training and to pitch you to appropriate venues over a 3-6 month contract, put a mark in #3 on the very outside close to the next level.

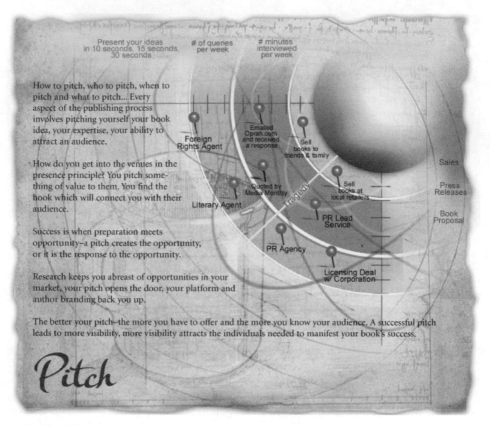

Present your ideas
in 10 seconds, 15 seconds,
30 seconds

\# of queries
per week

\# minutes
interviewed
per week

How to pitch, who to pitch, when to pitch and what to pitch... Every aspect of the publishing process involves pitching yourself your book idea, your expertise, your ability to attract an audience.

How do you get into the venues in the presence principle? You pitch something of value to them. You find the hook which will connect you with their audience.

Success is when preparation meets opportunity—a pitch creates the opportunity, or it is the response to the opportunity.

Research keeps you abreast of opportunities in your market, your pitch opens the door, your platform and author branding back you up.

The better your pitch—the more you have to offer and the more you know your audience. A successful pitch leads to more visibility, more visibility attracts the individuals needed to manifest your book's success.

Foreign
Rights Agent

Emailed
Oprah.com
and received
a response

Sell
books to
friends & family

Quoted by
Media Monthly

Sell
books at
local retailers

Literary Agent

PR Lead
Service

PR Agency

Licensing Deal
w/ Corporation

Tragedy

Sales

Press
Releases

Book
Proposal

Pitch

Sadly, the one shortcut to pitching is through tragedy, which brings the media *to* you, clamoring for your attention and story. Obviously, no one wants to undergo a tragedy just to write and pro mote a book, but using a tragedy to write a book that pays tribute or shows a way to help others heal from trauma or catastrophe, can be a powerful media magnet.

Pitch Principle Resources

· AuthorsCompanion.com has products and PR consulting services to help you hone your pitch and provides strategies for pitching proactively and reactively.

· ProfNet.com, or the simpler repackaged offering PRLeads.com, both send you media opportunities, it's up to you to respond providing exactly what the reporter or producer may need.

Publish Principle

In looking at the four levels, you have probably noticed that the further out from the center you go, the further along you are on the publishing path. Your writing ability is more developed, your platform larger, your pitches more succinct and relevant, and your media savvy greater. Now you are ready to look at your options for publishing.

Measure Publish Principle

How much energy have you put (or are you prepared to put) into the Publish Principle? Put a mark on the Chart in the **bottom right** quadrant.

PR investment:
1. How much money are you prepared to invest in PR? If it's under $1000, put a mark in #1. If it's between $1000-$2500, put a mark in #2. If between $2500-$5000, put a mark in #3, and if between $5000-$15,000 put a mark in #4.

2. What is your dream Advance—the money a major publisher will pay you upfront for your book idea, to be deducted from future sales? If you expect an advance or $1000-$2000, put a mark in #3; if it is $5000 -$50,000+, put a mark in #4.

Notice if the amount of money you are prepared to invest in PR matches the amount of money you expect for an advance—because that's exactly what publishers want you to spend it on—PR!

Expected Sales:
1. How many books do you expect to sell in the first year? If it's under 100 put a mark in #1; if it's between 100-1000 put a mark in #2; it it's between 1000 and 25,000 put a mark in #3; and if it's from 25,000 up to J.K. Rowling, put a mark in #4.

Evaluate your Chart

When you take a measured look at the 4 principles so far, then you are ready to apply the fourth principle. Take a good look at your marks. Are they concentrated more in one section than another?

Imagine a string connecting each mark, circling the center, spinning around like electrons around a nucleus. How far does your "author atom" expand? Now it is time to revisit the core . Ask yourself again, what is my intention in publishing this book? If you are passionate about your topic, an avid writer, and risk-taker, chances are what you have in front of you will be a glowing mass of efforts circling way out to the third and fourth levels.

Now quantify yourself in each of the principles. Then, based on your reach, choose your publishing option. The following pages describe the options for each level. You can choose your option to match your current markings, *or* you can focus more energy on each principle, and see how the laws of the Universe react as your book molecule expands.

The Science

Imagine this bundle of energy made of all your efforts becoming magnetized and attracting the connections and resources you need. Remember the positivity surrounding your core? You will be met with the same positive energy as you put out.

Now imagine how something you've written, or something you have left behind (a business card or bookmark), or a pitch you have made—which, while seemingly unsuccessful at the time, could get caught in the trajectory of your spiraling energy and make a connection somewhere else in the future. Imagine all of your efforts connecting, each one networking you to another great lead, sale or appearance. This is the chemistry—the actual transformation of the base idea to gold, and your book to profit. When your efforts reach critical mass and you create a nuclear chain reaction you create a Bestseller!

4 Publishing Options

Level #1 — Blue

Perhaps your publishing dreams aren't as grandiose as some of the other levels. Maybe you just want to give books to friends and family, and not spend any money on PR.

An **Author Service company** charges fees for each piece of the process from editing to basic book design and marketing services. They assign their ISBN, their name is on your book, they take a percentage of profit from retail, and mark up the books they sell to you (which is where they make a lot of profit.) Some well-known author service companies include: AuthorHouse, Aventine Press, Black Forest Press, Booklocker.com, BookPublisher, Cold Tree Press, Dog Ear Publishing, First Books, Infinity Publishing, iUniverse, Llumina Press, LuLu, Morgan James Publishing, Outskirts Press, PageFree Publishing, Publish America, SelfPublishing.com, Tabby House, Trafford Publishing, Universal Publishers, Unlimited Publishing, Virtualbookworm.com, WinePress Publishing, and Xlibris.

Though I don't endorse them, these companies are fine, and their services are fine. The drawbacks are 1) they take a percentage of your sales and mark up the cost of books; 2) they use a middleman you could use yourself; and 3) their name on your book leaves the stigma that you paid that company for an ISBN number and print-on-demand distribution.

Level #2 Red

A small independent press is the option for this level. If you know what a platform is, but haven't grown a huge one yet, this level is a great starting point for the first-time author. This, in essence, is YOU self-publishing.

The difference between publishing yourself and paying one of the author service companies in Level #1 is the owner of the ISBN. When it is your name on the spine (*the name you assign your own publishing entity which sounds like the perfect niche publisher for your book*), you collect 100% of the money directly and benefit from the brand you build.

When you self-publish you do not have to print a large press run of 1000-2000 books—in fact it is silly to do so before you have them sold! Using Ingram's Lightning Source print-on-demand company you can print as few or as many as you need. (This is the *same* printer the author service companies in Level #1 use.) Lightning will also distribute — meaning all of the retail sales for Amazon.com, BarnesandNoble.com, Target.com, Walmart.com and Ingram bookstore orders are filled automatically behind the scenes. You just collect the money!

Download the **Become Your Own Publisher Handbook** at www.wymacpublishing.com/BYOPabib.pdf for complete instructions. Here's a brief synopsis:

Step 1 - Name your publishing company and create an icon, and a brand you can be proud of.

Step 2 - Purchase an ISBN logbook at ISBN.org

Step 3 - Hire a publishing consultant, or use our BYOP Handbook to walk you through all of the publishing registrations.

Step 4 - Hire a book designer to create a powerful cover, back and spine and a professional interior layout. Use a professional who can get your files to perfect specifications.

Step 5 - Get an account with Lightning Source and have your designer upload files. Your book will appear on Amazon and all the other online retailers as well as available for special order through bookstores.

Become an Imprint!

Becoming an imprint of a larger publishing house is the ideal scenario for a new indie press to get launched. You will benefit from the brand that has already been built by the main "umbrella" publisher, yet you will maintain control of the revenue, still have your brand's name on the book, and can also create additional revenue by publishing others in your market under your imprint.

Wyatt-MacKenzie's Custom Imprint Program was launched in 2007 and has exceeded all of the imprint authors' expectations. It is a revolutionary transparent model aimed to empower authors. Visit www.wymacpublishing.com for details.

Level #3 Orange

The ideal publisher for this level is an established, medium size indie press in your niche that has bookstore distribution (instead of print on-demand.) Your manuscript should be professionally edited, and you should have an established platform and be ready to prove how you can reach it in a comprehensive marketing plan. They will print a run of 3,000-10,000 books, and possibly even offer a small advance.

The way to find the perfect indie press for your book is by researching who publishes the best books in your niche, someone who is known for reaching your specific market. Wyatt-MacKenzie for example focuses on mom writers and many of the authors in this book found us this way. Find a publisher that fits you, your niche, or your book, then follow their submission guidelines to the closest detail. This is where your writing craft, your platform and author branding, and your ability to pitch all come together! And, this is where all of your energy connects—when you pitch a publisher or acquisitions editor who has read about you or your work.

Level #4 Yellow

Level 4 is the stratosphere of the publishing universe. If you're looking to land a major publishing deal you'll need an agent to pitch your book idea. Advances are proportional to your platform, an assigned editor may rework content, and an assigned designer will package the book based on the marketing department's instructions.

Find literary agents and medium-to-large publishers in *Writer's Market*. Or look in the acknowledgements of books in your niche to find an agent who is thanked, google them, and approach through the proper channel with this connection as part of your pitch. You can also subscribe to *Publishers Marketplace* online to see who's getting publishing deals, how big they are, and who was the agent. Stay on top of *Publisher's Weekly* for book news in your industry. And good luck!

Here's a list of **major** publishing houses and *their* imprints:

Random House
> Bantam Dell
> Ballantine
> Crown
> Harmony
> Doubleday Broadway
> Knopf

Simon & Schuster
> Prentice Hall
> Pocket Books
> Wall Street Journal Books
> Fireside
> Touchstone

HarperCollins
> HarperBusiness
> HarperResource
> Perennial Currents
> Regan Books
> William Morrow

Holtzbrinck
> Macmillan
> Farrar, Straus & Giroux
> Henry Holt
> Picador
> St. Martin's Press
> St. Martin's Griffin
> Hill & Wang
> Times Books
> Metropolitan Books
> Faber & Faber
> North Point Press
> Owl Books
> Penguin Group

Berkley Books
> Dutton
> Gotham Books
> Penguin
> Plume
> G.P. Putnam's Sons
> Riverhead
> Jeremy P. Tarcher
> Viking

Time Warner
> Aspect
> Little, Brown and Co.
> Warner Vision

Harcourt
> Harcourt Trade
> Greenwood Publishing
> Holt, Rinehart and Winston
> Heinemann-Raintree

Houghton Mifflin
> Clarion Books
> Mariner Books

*List from *Smart Women Publish!*, Jan B. King, p.49,

What to do Next...

Now you know the secrets and science behind getting published. It is my hope, and my personal mission, that you will continue to spread this information to other writers, create support groups, and successfully get published. Here are some steps you can take next.

· Host the online **Secrets & Science to Getting Published Class**
www.abookisborn.com/hostsecretclass.html

· Start your own **A Book is Born** *Publishing* **Book Club**
www.abookisborn.com/bookclub.html

· Find an Author Support Group or Publishing Mentor
www.abookisborn.com/authorsupport.html

· **Start an Imprint** for your school, church, community or cause.
www.wymacpublishing.com/imprint.html

· If this is a hardcover edition there could be a **$1000 Certificate**
in the book jacket for you to redeem on Wyatt-MacKenzie premium
author branding services or our imprint program. If it is a paperback,
use the code "ABIB" to save $100 off any service we offer.

· Check out the *A Book is Born* **Book Trailer** on YouTube.com and
leave your comments.

· Post your review of this book on Amazon.com.

· Enter **A Book is Born TV Video Book Pitch Competition!**
Watch **www.abookisbornTV.com** for applications and details.
Writers are invited to shoot a 30-second video book pitch and post
on YouTube.com. Chosen winners receive a publishing contract and
$3000 author branding & marketing package, and will be asked to
keep a video diary throughout the publishing process.

· *What's next for Wyatt-MacKenzie, and maybe for you...*

APPENDIX

*"May the grace of knowing
how important your message is
surround you always."*

~ CHRISTINE LOUISE HOHLBAUM
author of *DIary of a Mother* and *SAHM I Am*

Resources

ON WRITING

Mama Writer: How to Raise a Writing Career Alongside Your Kids by Christina Katz

Writing Motherhood: Tapping Into Your Creativity as a Mother and a Writer by Lisa Garrigues

www.AbsoluteWrite.com

EDITING, GHOSTWRITING, PROOFREADING, INDEXING

Jenny Meadows, Copyediting and Proofreading Service, www.mycopyeditor.com, jenny@mycopyeditor.com, (512) 495-9550

Bernie Panitch, Proofreading and Copyediting, Verbatim Editing, LLC, verbatimproofreading@comcast.net, (973) 228-6520

Kim Pearson, Ghostwriting, Editing, Writing Coaching, Writing Classes www.primary-sources.com, (425) 865-0409

Gina Gerboth, Pueblo Indexing and Publishing Services www.puebloindexing.com, puebloindexing@gmail, (719) 562-0262

ON PUBLISHING

The Complete Idiot's Guide to Getting Published by Sheree Bykofsky and Jennifer Bayse Sander

The Complete Idiot's Guide To Self-Publishing by Jennifer Basye Sander

The Secret to Publishing Online Class:
www.wymacpublishing.com/thesecret.html

FIND AN AGENT

Writer's Market (Writer's Digest Books)
www.publishersmarketplace.com

BESTSELLER STORIES

The Making of a Bestseller by Brian Hill and Dee Power
Inside the Bestsellers by Jerrold Jenkins and Mardi Link

PUBLISHING LAW

Handbook of Publishing Law by Jonathan Kirsch
A Business Guide to Copyright Law by Woody Young

BOOK & AUTHOR PROMOTION

The Savvy Author's Guide to Book Publicity by Lissa Warren

Bestseller in 30 Days by Fern Reiss, and www. publishinggame.com

1001 Ways to Market Your Book by John Kremer, and www.book-marketing.com

The Frugal Book Promoter by Carolyn Howard-Johnson

Jump Start Your Book Sales by Marilyn & Tom Ross

The Author's Companion CD-Rom by Christine Louise Hohlbaum

www.amarketingexpert.com

www.experts.com

www.profnet.com/www.prleads.com

www.presskit247.com

www.publicityhound.com

www.PRWeb.com

ASSOCIATIONS

Publishers Marketing Association, www.pma-online.org

The Authors Guild, www.authorsguild.org

SPAN, www.spannet.org

INDUSTRY PUBLICATIONS
and links for book review submissions

Publishers Weekly
www.publishersweekly.com/article/CA6428088.html

Library Journal
www.libraryjournal.com/info/CA6415258.html

ALA Booklist
www.ala.org/ala/booklist/insidebooklist/booklistproc/proceduressubmitting.htm

Kirkus Reviews
www.kirkusreviews.com/kirkusreviews/about_us/submission.jsp

ForeWord Magazine
www.forewordmagazine.com/reviews/guidelines.aspx

PUBLICATIONS FOR MOM WRITERS

Brain, Child magazine, www.brainchildmag.com

Mom Writer's Literary Magazine, www.momwriterslitmag.com

Co-Author Bios & Books

Leeda Bacon

Leeda's compassionate encouragement is shared in *Be Ye Encouraged!* to help readers on their journey of weight reduction and making healthy choices. Leeda believes that you will be successful in achieving your dreams and beginning an exciting new chapter in your life. A shining example of her own philosophy, Leeda is on mission to inspire successful business women to be successful in their diet dreams.

Leeda is a native Californian, and resides in Sacramento. Married to her high school sweetheart, Stan, for 35 years, she has two wonderful children, Ian and Amy, a beautiful daughter-in-law, Melissa and caring son-in-law, Ryan. The light of her world are her eight grandchildren. Leeda has been involved in Bible Study Fellowship for 15 years and worked as a Funeral Arranger, serving families in their time of need, comforting and guiding them through that difficult time.

www.LeedaBacon.com

Christie G. Crowder

Christie has been a sounding board for young women, mothers, and aspiring entrepreneurs for almost a decade. Her passion for helping others achieve their life and business goals prompted her to restructure her former project management company to become CGC Connections, a thriving coaching firm for life enrichment. To enhance her skills, she trained to be a Life Enrichment Professional through the Inspiration Institute at Inspired Imaginations, LLC. She is now certified to coach individuals and lead community groups based on its licensed material.

In addition to her debut release *Your Big Sister's Guide to Surviving College*, Christie also contributes to online forums and print magazines for women, parents, and teens.

Christie lives with her husband, Curtis, their 3 year-old daughter, Kennedy, and brand new baby boy, Jackson, in the suburbs of Atlanta, Georgia. She is also working on the next installment of what she hopes to be an on-going series of Your Big Sister Guides.

www.YourBigSisterGuides.com

Kelley Cunningham

Kelley Cunningham is a syndicated humor writer and has been a contributor to *The Funny Times, Mothering* and *Brain, Child* magazines. Her monthly column, on which her book *What's The Matter With Mommy?* is based, was syndicated on the popular webzines imperfectparent.com and Quirkee.com. Kelley is also an award-winning fine artist and an illustrator of children's books, magazine covers and articles, and book covers for leading publishers. She was an art director for ten years at a number of New York advertising agencies and currently serves as art director at a major children's magazine. **www.KelleysArt.com**

Nina Marie Duran

At 24 years old, Nina has a Masters in Communication Arts, served as an intern with the San Antonio Spurs and KENS5, became an associate producer for *Great Day SA*, while also free-lancing for *City Pages* of San Antonio, serving as a regular journalist for *La Prensa*, and writing for Incarnate Word's Logos. With all of these accomplishments Nina is most proud of being mother to Elijah, her son. *Elijah on my Mind* is her personal experience as a young mom, embracing every opportunity. **www.ninamarieduran.com**

Maureen Focht

Maureen is the author of *Silent Heroes*, an educator for the Family-to-Family program with the National Alliance for the Mentally Ill, and a training specialist for the nationally known "Parent Project" program. Through her work with foster children, distressed families, and her own experience she writes about in her new book, she knows the traumas families face, and hopes to help families find understanding and healing. She holds a Masters degree in Educational Counseling from National University in Sacramento, California.

A business background and education gives Maureen unique insight in her involvement with Hand-to-Hand Mentoring, a program assisting single mothers to become self sufficient, productive members of the workforce through financial and career counseling. In addition, Maureen Focht is a court-appointed Special Advocate, and mentors foster children through court proceedings for educational and placement issues. Her extensive specialized training for this position focuses on the needs of abused and neglected children. Maureen's work in this sphere is also informed by her M.S. in Educational Counseling in 2002; her thesis topic was "Effects of Maternal Depression on School Age Children." **www.maureenfocht.com**

Norma Garcia

After losing her daughter in 2001 in a car accident, Norma made educating the public about organ and tissue donation her new journey and passion in life. She has served on the National Donor Memorial Advisory Committee for UNOS (United Network for Organ Sharing) and assisted in the design of the memorial in Richmond, VA; honoring America's donor families. In 2003 Norma and her family represented San Antonio, TX at the National Kidney Foundation Olympic Games at Disney World in Orlando, FL. In 2004 she was invited to be a keynote speaker at a fundraiser given in Palm Springs, Florida to benefit the National Donor Memorial.

Norma also serves her local community by being a volunteer & speaker for TOSA (Texas Organ Sharing Alliance). She has shared her compelling story in *My Dear Jasmine* of the gift of life to an overwhelming number of audiences. She has made an enormous contribution with her story to the medical community, bringing encouragement and a new sense of passion to the best practices classes on organ and tissue donation staff in local hospitals.

Samantha Gianulis

Samantha writes from southern California where she has lived for thirty-one years. After leaving the catering and event planning industry in 1999 to be a full-time mom, she missed food and camaraderie. *Little Grapes on the Vine* is Sam's sparkling return to the food world combined with her mommy world.

These days she's a senior editor at momwriterslitmag.com where she has a column, "Making It Up as I Go Along." She has been published in *San Diego Family Magazine, Hybrid Mom Magazine, Mommyhood Diaries: Living the Chaos One Day at a Time*, on Parents.com, recipestoday.com, longstoryshort.us and sandiegomama.com. Raising her children to be wholehearted foodies like her, Samantha and her family can often be found eating seafood by the ocean in their search for the perfect coastal culinary experience. **www.SamanthaGianulis.com**

Caron Goode

Caron, a nationally certified and licensed professional counselor, has published numerous books besides *The Art & Science of Coaching Parents Successfully* and contributes articles regularly to parenting publications. Caron draws her insights from over fifteen years in private psychotherapy practice and thirty years' experience in the fields of education, personal empowerment, and therapy. These professional and her personal experiences as a parent create Caron's refreshing and unique parenting approach, grounded in science yet easy and practical for parents to follow.

Caron, with her husband Tom Goode, ND, currently manages and directs the International Breath Institute, an educational and training organization that offers health and lifestyle management seminars and certification. She and her husband live in Tucson, Arizona. She is the mother of one daughter. **www.inspiredparenting.net**

Christine Louise Hohlbaum

Since March 2004, Christine has been a creative PR consultant for book authors and small businesses. Her popular on-line course has helped authors of all stripes gain national attention. She later turned the course into her CD-Rom, *The Author's Companion*. She is a founding member of the Mom-Writers Publishing Cooperative with her book *SAHM I Am*, which was published in both English and German. Formerly, she consulted with a Virgina PR firm, she currently works as a PR writer for one of the top firms in the US, Wasabi Publicity.

When she isn't networking, doing public speaking, writing, or wiping up messes, Christine generally likes to frolic with her husband and two children in their home near Munich, Germany. **www.sahmiam.com**, **www.authorscompanion.com**

Terilee Harrison

A former small town Ohio girl now living near Los Angeles, Terilee is the proud wife of Terry and mom to Jackie and Cole. Through her work building and expanding RBN (the Relationship Building Network), Terilee has developed and enhanced her own networking skills.

Previously a corporate mom turned mom entrepreneur, Terilee realized moms face unique challenges and have few resources solely dedicated to helping them as they juggle their business and raise their family so she wrote *The Business Mom Guide Book*.

Combining her passion for helping other moms with a fearless life, Terilee now spends her days networking not only in Los Angeles, but with mom business owners around the world. **www.thebusinessmom.com**

Deborah Hurley

Abandonment, extreme phobias throughout her adolescent years, and childbirth in her late twenties paved the way for a relentless, life-threatening condition that consumed Deborah's mind and body. She speaks candidly about what it felt like to have lost the ability to feel, think, want, give and love and how she fought desperately to live for the sake of her children.

Born and raised on Eastern Long Island, Deborah spent most of her life dancing and teaching young girls. She was an ambitious teen who loved to write to presidents, authors, teachers and newspapers. In 2006 she combined her love for writing with a ten-year battle over depression to create her inspiring and candid book *Fragments of Hope*. **www.FragmentsofHope.com**

Jennifer Kalita

Jennifer Kalita has been a communications and business consultant, writer, speaker, and strategist for more than a decade. She empowers entrepreneurs to live a life In Business and In Balance™ with her book *The Home Office Parent*, and has educated thousands of entrepreneurs in all facets of business launch, development, and promotion. She is the founder and CEO of The Kalita Group and Strategic Women (strategicwomen.com); Boomer Buzz PR columnist at Second50Years.com; and author of numerous books and business development programs. **www.thekalitagroup.com**

Marna Krajeski

Marna Krajeski, author of *Household Baggage: The Moving Life of a Soldier's Wife*, is a professional writer and Army wife of sixteen years. Before that, she was on active duty as an Army helicopter pilot. She has degrees in English from The College of William and Mary and Austin Peay State University. Her articles and essays about military life have appeared in numerous periodicals, including *Off Duty, Married to the Military, American Baby, Army Times*, and *The Providence Journal*.

Krajeski taught writing at the University of Rhode Island, where her husband chaired the ROTC department. They have two children, Elena and Stephen.
www.householdbaggage.com

Pamela Jo Leo

The mother of two grown daughters and grandmother of three, Pam has been working with families for more than thirty years as a childcare provider, parent educator, childbirth educator, doula, grief work facilitator, and parent mentor. With a passion for learning, teaching, and writing about optimal human development Pam has been the "Empowered Parents" columnist for the *Parent & Family* paper in Maine for the last ten years and finally penned her award-winning book *Connection Parenting* in 2005. Pam is also a founding member of the Alliance for Transforming the Lives of Children. **www.ConnectionParenting.com**

Kathryn Mahoney

Kathryn has been entertaining friends and family with her writing for years. But, it wasn't until 2001 when Kathryn decided to share her cracked view of life with the rest of the world. She submitted a couple of columns to her local newspaper and lo and behold, the editor liked them. Kathryn started writing, "Sunny Side Up", for Nashoba Publishing in 2001 and continues to write for them today. Kathryn's book, *Cracked at Birth: One Madcap Mom's Thoughts on Motherhood, Marriage & Burnt Meatloaf* is an anthology of her columns that readers have come to know and love.

Prior to launching her humor writing career, Kathryn put her creative talent to good use in the marketing arena for many years and now runs her own business, CreativEdge Marketing Communications.

When she's not writing her column or juggling the demands of her business, Kathryn is busy raising her two young sons with her husband in Groton, Massachusetts. **www.CrackedatBirth.com**

Alana Morales

When she is not chasing after her kids, Alana Morales manages to find time to write. Her book *Domestically Challenged* is a humorous guide book for all moms.

Alana received a Bachelors degree in Psychology from Arizona State University and went on to teach English for six years before staying home with her kids. She began her writing career with a parenting humor column, which she still writes to this day. Alana hosted the online radio show Mom Writer's Talk Radio and currently runs a copywriting business called The Write Decision. When she is not volunteering in her son's classroom or trying to potty train a reluctant toddler, she also teaches an online class for new at-home parents.

Alana resides in Arizona with her two very active kids and husband of ten years. **www.AlanaMorales.com**

Victoria Pericon

Victoria is a family lifestyle correspondent on national television and editor of Savvy Mommy magazine, the award-winning resource devoted to providing parents of children under six ith product and service reviews. She appears on more than 200 television stations as Savvy Mommy and has been quoted in over 300 publications.

Victoria has also had the opportunity to interview some of the most accomplished women in business and entertainment. Her acclaimed first book, *Mommy Land: Entering the Insanity of Motherhood*, is a satire about motherhood in America. Victoria lives in Manhattan with her three children. **www.SavvyMommy.com**

Caroline Poser

Caroline Poser is the mother of three sons in Groton, Massachusetts. *MotherMorphosis* chronicles her first two and a half years of motherhood, when Caroline was juggling a work-at-home career as a technology writer with the brand-new role of mommy to two under two. She put pen to paper (and sticky note, napkin, and sometimes church bulletin) in an effort to regain and retain her sanity. Today she is employed in corporate America as a technology sales professional and is writing another book called *Snakes, Snails, and Puppy-dog Tales*. **www.MotherMorphosis.com**

Malonda Richard

As an author, host, spokeswoman and model, Malonda Richard communicates with a powerful, natural ability. From 1999-2001, she earned her following as former host of BET: Next and Out the Box. Her book *My Life Isn't Perfect...But Thank God My Baby Is* provides a raw glimpse inside single motherhood. Today, Malonda is the founder of MamiHood.com, a website dedicated to supporting and empowering single mothers. Malonda and her daughter Ameerah reside in Brooklyn, New York. **www.MalondaRichard.com**

Paula Schmitt

Paula is the award-winning author of *Living in a Locker Room: A Mom's Tale of Survival in a Houseful of Boys*, a radio talk show host, columnist, and founder of Mom Writer's Productions, LLC which she created for mom writers and authors. Her mission is to help moms who want to start writing, accomplish their goals and be published. Paula believes all mothers have something important to say and should be heard.

Paula is the host of the What Did You Do All Day? podcast, and Founder/President and Editor of *Mom Writer's Literary magazine*, an award-winning online quarterly publication for mom writers and authors. She was also the creator and host of Mom Writer's Talk Radio, a radio talk show for moms.

The mother of five children, Ms. Schmitt lives in Vermont with her family. **www.PaulaSchmitt.com**

Julie Watson Smith

Julie is dedicated to inspiring mommy well-being by providing tools and support to organize, prioritize, and energize while managing and even accepting the chaos of mommyhood.

Proud wife, mother of three, entrepreneur, writer, reigning chaos queen, and author of *Mommyhood Diaries*, Julie relinquished the dream of perfection and now lives comfortably in the chaos, one day at a time.

Julie is the founder and owner of Mommy Hullabaloo, a life management company dedicated to inspiring moms while learning, living, and loving the chaos of mommyhood. Additionally, Julie pens a humorous parenting column of the same name. **www.mommyhullabaloo.com**

Arlene Schusteff

Arlene's work has appeared in a host of publications. She first realized the power of the pen when she was eight and an essay she wrote won her a backstage pass to meet The Jackson 5.

Arlene's book *Peanut Butter, Playdates & Prozac* takes a hysterical look at the lifestyle choices of moms today. She lives with her husband Howard, and children, Rachel and Jake, in a suburb of Chicago. When she's not writing, she spends most of her time searching for the lost remote control and trying to get motivated to organize ten years of family photos. **www.ArleneSchusteff.com**

Jennifer Thie

At the age of seven, still unable to read or write, Jennifer was diagnosed dyslexic. With determination and the love and support of her family, Jennifer would conquer academics, athletics, marriage and motherhood with great success, albeit with many struggles and losses. Her first book *And Then...Came Arthur* chronicles her search for spirituality and meaning during the emotional highs and lows surrounding the birth of her twins.

Jennifer Thie lives with her husband, two children, two dogs and three cats where she was raised in Palo Alto, California. **www.JenniferThie.com**

Iris Waichler

Iris has a Master Degree in Social Work and had been practicing for over 25 years when she authored *Riding the Infertility Roller Coaster*. She worked as a Medical Social Worker in large teaching hospitals in the Chicago area for thirteen years, and was Director of Medical Social Work at Glenbrook Hospital.

Iris has a wealth of experience working with infertility, rehabilitation, cancer, and emergency room patients. She has done work leading a Pregnant at Last (PAL) group, doing peer counseling, and volunteering on the hotline for RESOLVE, as well as authoring many articles for RESOLVE.

Iris Waichler lives in Chicago with her husband, Steve, and her daughter, Grace. **www.InfertilityRollerCoaster.com**

About the Author

Nancy C. Cleary

Nancy grew up in Massachusetts and had a passion for art from a very young age. She studied visual communications at DeCordova, Parsons, and Rhode Island School of Design during high school and earned a BFA in Graphic Design from RISD in 1990. After graduation Nancy traveled across the country to San Diego and landed an art director position for Robert Allen's "No Money Down" real estate seminar company. A short year there was followed by a year with a multimedia company in Carlsbad, California whose biggest client was Anthony Robbins—Nancy had the incredible opportunity of working behind the scenes at his Maui events and yes, even walked across hot coals.

Then she followed her heart and spirit to Oregon where she launched a graphic design studio in 1992 and helped her partner start his own publishing company. Nancy beautifully branded the small press and sent breathtaking proposals to clients that included: His Holiness The Dalai Lama of Tibet, Tara Singh, Coretta Scott King, Ken Blanchard, Richard Bach, Kenny Loggins and Karl Anthony. That year Nancy also met the cowboy who would inspire her to settle in Deadwood, and later start a family—Wyatt was born in 1997 and MacKenzie in 1998. When Nancy began to feel her graphic design work wasn't important enough to pull her away from her kids so much she searched for something "more." It was then she decided to launch her own publishing company, and named it after them.

As Nancy collaborated with mom writers and entrepreneurs she discovered a very special niche—which needed her talent. The ability to empower these moms—to increase their brand equity—was the most fulfilling work she had found thus far in her career. Cleary produced dozens of publications from 2000-2004 including *The Best of Mom's Business Magazine*, *I Love My Life: A Mom's Guide to Working from Home*, *Mom's Work-at-Home Kit and Workbook*, and *Today's BlueSuitMom Magazine*.

In 2004 Wyatt-MacKenzie signed Jen Singer for *14 Hours 'Til Bedtime*, and based on the success of this traditionally published title, Nancy created the blueprint for the Mom Writer's Publishing Cooperative. Through 2005 to 2007 Nancy published 24 co-op titles, many receiving national acclaim and garnering numerous independent book awards.

As 2008 begins Nancy plans to focus on her brand new imprint model, which is truly a unique offering in the industry, as well as reviewing book proposals for her traditional model. Nancy's dream of an author's retreat where writers go to get published and learn about the process firsthand has a goal for completion in 2010.

Acknowledgements

Thank you to all of my co-authors for your heartfelt contributions.
I hope your words will go on to inspire many, many writers to pursue
their publishing dreams (*and buy your books!*)

Thank you to Jennifer Basye Sander for taking time in a busy schedule
to write the foreword.

Thank you to all the advance reviewers for your energy and enthusiasm,
you have driven me with your encouragement.

Thank you to Wyatt and MacKenzie who are the
inspiration for everything I do, for their patience when mom
works long hours in her "bubble."

And most of all, thank you to Joey,
without you none of this would be possible.
I love us.

Index

Wyatt-MacKenzie Publishing, Inc.
DEADWOOD, OREGON
www.WyMacPublishing.com

Wyatt-MacKenzie can help you on whichever publishing path fits your talent and aspirations best. The publishing journey can be a challenging one – we empower our authors, helping them to build their platform and elevate their career, while inspiring their children. Here are some of our current offerings.

Wyatt-MacKenzie Major Releases

If you have been published by a traditional publisher, have a proven sales record, a solid platform, a comprehensive marketing plan, a budget for professional PR, and a well-written, copyedited and researched book – send us your book proposal and we will schedule an interview. If your platform qualifies you for bookstore distribution we work with major distributor Perseus Books to reach bookstore buyers and reps 7 months ahead of your pub date. *Moderate advances are offered.*

Wyatt-MacKenzie Imprint Program

We have a brand new offering – the Custom Imprint is a completely new approach created in response to what authors have been asking for over the years. It is the perfect combination of our consulting, packaging, and branding for authors who want the control of self-publishing combined with the security of an established umbrella publisher and benefits of an in-house design and publicity team.

Author Support Groups, Publishing Clubs, Mentorship Programs

The Mom Writer's Publishing Co-Op is closed, but the members offer a variety of support groups and individual mentoring programs.

Publishing & Book Promotion Consulting

We can answer your questions about publishing, review publishing contracts, and assist authors in creating their pre-publication book marketing plan.

Author Branding

Our goal is to elevate your brand equity – to take the book you publish and the platform you build and package them together with creative marketing expertise that makes you irresistible to the media, customers, and all decision makers.